When Heroes Die

WHEN HEROES DIE

A forgotten archive reveals the last days of the schoolfriends who died for Britain

Sue Smart

breedon books
PUBLISHING

First published in Great Britain in 2001 by
The Breedon Books Publishing Company Limited
Breedon House, 3 The Parker Centre, Derby, DE21 4SZ.

ISBN 1 85983 256 3

Printed and bound by Butler & Tanner Ltd, Frome, Somerset
Cover printing by GreenShires Ltd, Leicester

Contents

For John and Isabel,
and in loving memory
of Olivia

Acknowledgements

THIS book began as a project to involve some of my pupils at Gresham's School in historical research and to bring a human face to our study of the First World War. It occured to me that for some of them, at the age of 13, the war must seem too big a topic to grasp imaginatively, and that the stories of young men who were their predecessors at Gresham's might illuminate it. These boys were, after all, earlier inhabitants of our same studies and classrooms, earlier actors in the theatre in the woods, earlier players on the cricket square. Most significantly, when they met their deaths, some were scarcely older than my pupils.

My colleague and friend Michael Barrett first told me of the remarkable collection of letters recorded in old school magazines, sent back from the war to the then headmaster, George Howson. It is to Michael that my thanks go in large measure for opening up this past Gresham's world.

For two years, on most Saturday mornings in "Hobbies" time, two enthusiastic and loyal research assistants, my pupils Harriet Baker and Jenna Hares, joined me in the school library. They listed names and regiments, wrote letters, and scoured the internet for leads to follow, and I thank them very much for their efforts. I hope they discovered that research is fun. I would also like to remember here my late colleague Belinda Fisher, who helped us and would have loved to see the outcome of our work.

As the picture began to come into focus, we grew more ambitious. We contacted relatives of the war dead, who generously shared with us family archives and reminiscences without which the book could not have come to life. David Boxall, Rob Roseveare, Bill Wynne Willson, Margaret Sharman and Jonathan Royds-Jones were vital to the making of the book, and I am most grateful to them.

After *The Sunday Times Magazine* published Richard Girling's excellent article entitled *The Lost Boys* in November 2000, more help came flooding in. I owe a debt of gratitude to the families of Adrian Graves, Alfred Hyde, Neill Newsum and Douglas Richardson for the information they let me publish about their predecessors. Many others wrote and e-mailed, too, to offer all sorts of information and photographs, and the text has been enriched by the contributions of Stuart Leslie, Robert Smith and Malcolm Cooper. I received over 300 letters, practical, touching, encouraging and informative, and to all my correspondents go my thanks. Any errors in the text are, of course, my own.

My colleagues have buoyed me up on the waves of their enthusiasm for the project, and I am grateful for the invaluable contributions of Roger Betts, David Hamill, Tony Leech and John Rayner. Steve Benson suggested the title and shared with me some wonderful source material. I have much relished our discussions. The Fishmongers' Company, the headmaster John Arkell, and the Old Greshamian Club all offered generous help. I am indebted to the Governors for their kind permission to use the material and photographs for which they hold the copyright. Ian Ormes has taken much of the administrative burden from me at times of crisis and Frances Chenevix-Trench helped greatly when I was sinking in a sea of correspondence.

My greatest and most loyal support has, of course, come from my family. My thanks to them go beyond words.

Introduction

ON A sunny summer afternoon, Saturday, 18 July 1914, the 1st XI cricket team at Gresham's School, Holt, took the field against the Old Boys. "The Cricket Season of 1914 was remarkable for the consistently fine weather, resulting in a perfect wicket," according to the school magazine, *The Gresham*. One surprising detail is that the scorecard shows that the 12th men on both sides actually played, making 24 on the field. The Old Boys declared their innings at 232 for 5, and the

8 *THE GRESHAM.*

MR. B. COZENS.-HARDY'S XI.

H. Cozens-Hardy, not out 67
G. S. Stevens,c Farmer, b Hawksley.......37
E. W. Cozens-Hardy, c Farmer b Graves 8
A. Theobald, lbw., b Graves... 8
M. W. Ireland, c Wells, b Laverack 1
W. A. Cook, lbw, b Laverack 9
S. O. Page, not out..............................55
S. Pick
J. B. Mahoney
B. Cozens-Hardy
R. J. Gowing
} did not bat.

Extras......7

Total (for 5 wkts). 193

GRESHAM'S SCHOOL *v.* MR. A. H. CARTER'S XI.

Played on July 14th.

GRESHAM'S SCHOOL.

J. H. C. Wooldridge, b Wilson..... 0
R. A. Fitzgerald, run out.....................38
D. W. Jacques, b Durrant.....................23
J. Jefferson, c Fishwick, b Durrant 15
J. A. Nicholson, c A. H. Carter, b Durrant 6
C. R. H. Farmer, b Hoff 12
A H. Graves, b Durrant 12
J. F. Laverack, b Hoff 1
C. H. Steven, b Durrant.......................11
C. N. Newsum, c Wells, b Durrant......... 8
O. Hawksley, not out 6
Extras 21

Total 153

MR. A. H. CARTER'S XI.

E. Wilson, b Farmer.......................... 2
H. G. Hoff, lbw, b Laverack 11
F. W. Wilson, b Jefferson 40
R. D. Carter, c Fitzgerald, b Farmer ...123
C. E. Durrant, st Steven, b Hawksley ... 4
W. H. Prosser, b Laverack 49
R. Wharton, c Graves, b Jacques 25
R. H. Partridge, c and b Farmer 43
T. F. Fishwick, b Farmer 19
A. H. Carter, not out 0
C. D. Wells, not out 0
Extras 19

Total 335

GRESHAM'S SCHOOL *v.* OLD BOYS.

Played on July 18th.

GRESHAM'S SCHOOL

J. H. C. Wooldridge, c Wright, b Barker 11
R. A. Fitzgerald, b Barker...... 8
D. W. Jacques, run out..... 28
J. Jefferson, c Hill, b Barker...... .... .18
C. R. H. Farmer, b Wright................ ...0
C. A. Hill, b Barker........... 49
J. A. Nicholson, c Newsum, b Cadge......23
C. N. Newsum, c Newsum, b Cadge.........4
A. H. Graves, hit wkt., b Rouse..............0
J. F. Laverack, c Newsum, b Cadge.........9
C. H. Stevens, hit wkt., b Rouse....... . 3
C. D. Wells, not out.............................36
Extras 13

Total 202

OLD BOYS.

H. W. Partridge, c Nicholson, b Farmer 14
R. H. Partridge, b Farmer........ 52
B. J. Cadge, c Steven, b Hill..................46
H. N. Newsum, c Fitzgerald, b Farmer 40
A. G. Wright, b Farmer.......................28
M. C. Hill, not out... 11
L. F. St. J. Davies, not out 25
W. J. Spurrell
M. E. B. Crosse
C. N. Barker
F. V. Jacques
C. V. Rouse
} did not bat

Extras..... 16

Total (for 5 wkts). 232

GRESHAM'S SCHOOL *v.* MR. J. R. ECCLES' XI.

Played on July 25th.

GRESHAM'S SCHOOL.

J. H. C. Wooldridge, b Cozens-Hardy ...17
R. A. Fitzgerald, b Evans..................... 2
D. W. Jacques, b Evans 8
J Jefferson, c Evans, b Cozens-Hardy ... 1
C. R. H. Farmer, lbw, b Smith 12
J. A. Nicholson, c Robertson, b Evans ... 7
A. H. Graves, b Smith 4
C. A. Hill, c Spurrell, b Evans... 1
J. F Laverack, b Smith............... 4
C. H. Steven, not out... 7
C. D. Wells, b Smith 2
Extras............. ... 6

Total.........71

The scorecard for the School v the Old Boys cricket match on 18 July 1914. By the end of the war, 11 of the 24 who took the field that day had lost their lives in war.

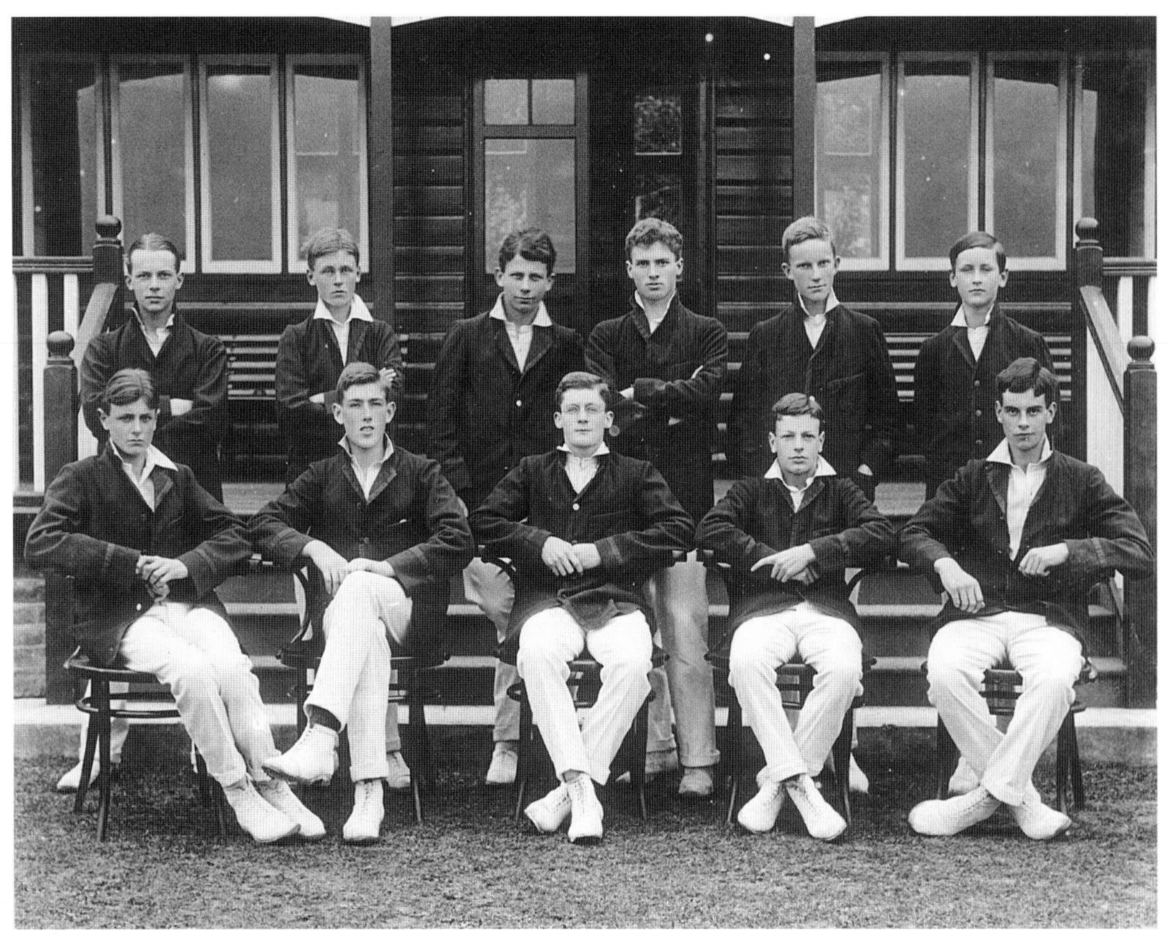

The School XI on 18 July. On the back row Douglas Wells (MC), (extreme left) John Nicholson, David Jacques and Cuthbert Hill (third, fourth and fifth from left) were killed in the war, as was Adrian Graves (MC and Bar) (seated, centre). The 12th man, Neill Newsum, is not pictured, but was also killed.

School in reply made only 202, thus losing by 30 runs. It was just one of seven defeats out of nine matches for the school that season, *The Gresham* blaming the lack of a fast bowler to operate on the hard sun-baked pitches.

The headmaster of Gresham's would not have been unduly concerned by the poor record of that season. He regarded games as a means of gaining healthy exercise and as an opportunity to exercise proper moral behaviour, but the fact of winning or losing was of little moment. His indifference to the actual game of cricket was total, his biographer, J. H. Simpson, recounting an amusing incident of a few years earlier:

> "I remember being asked, with some of my colleagues, to meet at dinner a rather distinguished visitor to the School House. 'Bad news from Australia, isn't it?' had begun the latter in a harmless attempt to make conversation, when he was brought up short by Howson's blank expression. It would be difficult to say which was

> the more surprised, the guest at finding a public schoolmaster who did not know that a Test Match was in progress, or his host at the idea of anyone of intelligence sparing a thought for so trivial a matter."

This cricket match was entirely unremarkable in every respect but one: its timing was momentous. Three weeks before, in distant Sarajevo in the Balkan province of Bosnia, Archduke Franz Ferdinand, the heir apparent to the throne of the Austro-Hungarian Empire, and his wife, Sophia, were assassinated by Gavrilo Princip, a 19-year-old Bosnian Serb who was fighting for the day when Bosnia would be part of Serbia. The repercussions of the double murder, in the context of European politics which had divided Europe into armed alliance systems, would lead directly to the early deaths of no fewer than 11 of the young men of Gresham's who walked out on to the school cricket field in rural North Norfolk on that fine Saturday in 1914.

Within a year Marlborough Crosse had fallen, the victim of a sniper, in the trenches of northern France. By mid-1916 two brothers, Cuthbert and Mark Hill,

The cricket pavilion at Gresham's School, pictured in the balmy days before the Great War devastated the school.

had lost their lives within six weeks of one another, Cuthbert at Jutland and Mark on the Somme. Noel Barker died instantly after being hit by a shell which fell directly on his dugout, and David Jacques was killed in the trenches of France by a sniper's shot to the head, at the end of 1916. During 1917, Robert Partridge was accidentally killed at Gaza and Neill Newsum died by shellfire in France. Adrian Graves fell in the spring of 1918 on Henin Hill, having held his position for a whole day with his machine-gunners against very strong German attacks. In the last months of the war Douglas Wells was killed while on patrol duty in the air, and John Nicholson died of wounds received in action in France. One day before the Armistice was signed, after weeks of work while he was fighting illness, Leslie Davies died, far from home, of malaria. These 11 represent only a fraction of the losses sustained by the school. In total, 100 Gresham's boys and one master were killed in the Great War. This is their story, and the story of a school in wartime.

The Last Dregs of Peace

IN THE summer of 1914 Gresham's was a school "on the up". During the 19th century, and indeed from its foundation as a grammar school in the reign of Mary Tudor, it had jogged along "usefully" but undramatically in the middle of the small market town of Holt in North Norfolk. Its most notorious event, the hanging of the schoolmaster outside his school in 1650, was, disappointingly, a legend, and the reality was much more prosaic. Although the school had strong links with Cambridge University and a minority pursued academic careers there, in 1900 fewer than 50 boys were receiving an old-fashioned grammar school education, which took them for the most part into careers in farming, in trade and only occasionally into the professions.

A turning point for Gresham's came with the Endowment Act of 1899, which re-formed the school and gave it public school status. Under the leadership of George Howson from September 1900, and on a large new site outside the town from 1903, vigorous changes could take place and they did – rapidly. Howson had been appointed, by accident it seems, to his previous teaching post at Uppingham. Misreading the telegram sent to him, he mistakenly turned up there for interview and was given the job. He pursued a sound but unremarkable career at Uppingham, but his chance to make his mark came in 1900. Howson arrived at Gresham's with a distinctive approach to schoolmastering, in which building character counted for much, while academic success, although laudable, counted for less, and prowess on the sports field counted for little indeed.

Nevertheless, the first decade of the 20th century saw the introduction of a modern curriculum and the building of an entirely new school. In 1903 the school, with its 114 pupils, moved from its original site in the middle of Holt to a spacious area about a mile up the Cromer Road, surrounded by fields and woodland. School House was run by Howson himself, helped by his two unmarried sisters, Rosa and Mary. By 1907, Howson could tell his Speech Day guests that school numbers stood at 182 and that with the boarding houses, Woodlands and Bengal Lodge, as well as School House (or "Headmaster's" as it

was customarily known), almost full, places would in future be filled by competitive examination. The huge gain in numbers was remarkable, as was the fact that the school was by now attracting boys from all over the country. The register reveals families based in London, in Sunderland, Nottingham and Herefordshire as well as the local roots of many more, from Norfolk, Suffolk and Lincolnshire. When the war came, for many Gresham's boys there was no such thing as a local regiment in Norfolk.

George Howson, headmaster of Gresham's School, photographed shortly after his appointment in 1900, when he was 40 years old.

Many of the boys who would be remembered for their valour in war were already making their names in *The Gresham* for their sporting, cultural and academic achievements. In a small school such names appeared again and again. These were the Gresham's "golden lads" – winning places at Oxford and Cambridge, breaking school athletics records, leading their fellows as school prefects, singing, acting, debating, shooting, with all the enthusiasm of those whose opportunities seemed boundless.

Dallas Wynne Willson, the housemaster of the Junior School, which occupied the former school building and was known then as now as the Old School House, recalled in his memoirs the atmosphere of those last days before the war:

> "In my diary I can find no mention of War until 27th July, the day that Austria declared war against Servia; (it was Servia then, written later Serbia). Again on Friday, 31st July, 'Bad war rumours. We may be involved', and on Sunday, 2nd August, 'great European tension – grave sermon by the Rector.' My diary tells of tennis parties and a cricket match, family news, comings and goings and little household details – in fact the last dregs of the full cup of those vanished Victorian-Edwardian pre-war years."

In terms of the development of the school, the great issue in 1914 was the chapel, begun in 1912 and by the beginning of the war appearing amid a forest of "unsightly" girders near the newest house, Farfield, which had been completed in the spring of 1911. In 1908, Howson had said at Speech Day:

> "Some months ago it was remarked to me that Gresham's School would not take the position due to it until it had a school chapel. I interpret the meaning of the remark that the strength and the life of the school lies in the reality of the religion of its members, and that strength and life must have a centre. A school chapel is the heart of a school."

A postcard showing the new Gresham's School, sent by a pupil, William Blatch, in 1906. He has marked the various buildings for the benefit of his family. In 1903 it was envisaged that Gresham's would remain mainly a day school, as the school buildings were designed for 300 pupils, but the boarding house for only 40.

By 1911, with the active support of the second master, J. R. Eccles, the necessary £2,500 had been collected to allow for the purchase of a site, and in the summer of the following year, amidst great ceremony, the foundation stone was laid. Conceived therefore as an essential focus of a Christian school, by 1916 when the chapel was consecrated, it would have taken on the character of a memorial.

In common with so many others, the boys of Gresham's School responded with alacrity to the call to arms. In their case, membership of the Cadet Corps was compulsory and taken seriously by Sergeant Steer who was a strong influence on the young John Reith. In his autobiography, Lord Reith speaks of Steer:

> "...an ex-colour sergeant of the Scots Guards... I developed an impressive 'word of command', became a sergeant and a good shot."

Steer was evidently a formidable figure. He departed Gresham's School for the colours in 1915, having lost his young son Charles, a drummer boy with the Scots Guards, early in the war. The school magazine recorded:

> "No one who was here when he first arrived will ever forget the way he electrified the Corps by his smartness. It was a familiar saying in those days that his salute could be *heard*."

"The Masters" photographed in 1908. Dallas Wynne Willson, the housemaster of the junior boys, is standing at the extreme left. He lived in the Old School House in the centre of Holt from 1905. J. R. Eccles, housemaster of Woodlands, flanks Howson to the left and John Chambré Miller, housemaster of Farfield, to the right.

Howson's reaction to war was more mixed. He was not militaristic, and while he was extremely proud of the patriotism of his boys, he nonetheless made clear his moral position. In an Open Letter in 1914 he began, "I detest war." By the end of 1918 he had 101 more specific reasons to detest it. But his letter went on to explain his belief that the war was inescapable and would be won for freedom and permanent peace for Europe. He commended with pride those boys who had not waited for commissions but who had joined the ranks so that they could make their contribution immediately. This provoked controversy. In the next edition of *The Gresham* a contributor pointed out that the great need was for officers "who have had even a little training, and the OTC was meant to provide officers. Besides, a Public School does give one a certain amount of training in leadership." Howson hastily corrected the impression he had previously given, saying that he had been successful in persuading several OGs to apply for commissions.

The public schools were seen traditionally as the natural seed-bed of officer material for Britain's professional army, and it was true that the Officers' Training

Corps, begun in 1907 by R. B. Haldane, the Secretary for War, had had as its intention the preparation of young officers for a possible war. In the first seven months of the war, the OTC created over 20,000 commissioned officers, some of them, like Dawson Atkin, Cosmo Duff-Gordon and Douglas Wells, going to their regiments straight from school.

It is difficult to imagine Howson's concept of war from a 21st-century standpoint. The gulf between his thinking and ours is profound. In his time, the last wars fought by the British Army had been in Afghanistan, the Sudan and South Africa, all faraway, even exotic places. They were fought on horseback, with rifles and bayonets, and casualties were counted in hundreds, not thousands. War was glorified in the popular literature read by the boys – the novels of G. A. Henty and stories in *The Boys' Own Paper* for example – and honour was the goal of every fighting man. It was a persistent myth. Howson could, of course, have known nothing of the hell of total war that was to come, any more than his boys could; of battles lasting months not days, of artillery bombardments and lethal shrapnel, of ceaseless noise, of filth and mud and unburied corpses. Unknowingly, Howson was encouraging his boys to a role of greatest danger: although it is not possible to be certain of the figures, the death toll for officers may have been as much as 27 per cent, against an average rate of 12 per cent for all deaths of men in the war. (Denis Winter, *Death's Men*)

The beginning of the war was attended by great excitement in Holt. Wynne Willson's memoirs vividly evoke the preparations for, moreover the hopes of, action:

> "I note that the weather on Tuesday, 4th August was showery in the afternoon. About midnight I went out into the town to Rounce and Wortley's Stationery Shop, where news was to be posted. It came from Cromer by a motor-cyclist, one of our day-boys. It was read out – the fateful message that England had declared war against Germany at 11pm. There was a crowd in the street and an outburst of cheering, and I remember our school doctor shouting, 'Don't cheer, you don't know what you are in for!' All that night there was noise and excitement: boy scouts were cycling about calling up reservists and territorials…
>
> Wednesday (an extra Bank Holiday) was showery and thundery. A day of rumours – unrest. We expected a naval battle off our coast! My brother-in-law and I went up, late at night, to the high fire-staircases on our new buildings and listened for the noise of guns at sea, and we almost persuaded ourselves that we could hear them.

So strong were the rumours of a naval battle the next day that Miller (Housemaster of Farfield) and I summoned all the principal people of Holt to a meeting in my school dining hall that day to arrange for reception of the wounded. I was elected Chairman and we formed a number of committees for transport, ambulance work etc., and arranged for the loan of beds, bedding and other necessaries, and the next day I telegraphed to the Governors of the School (the Headmaster had gone away and we could not get at him) and obtained permission to use the school dormitories for temporary hospitals!

The Old School House. The building dates from the 1850s, but stands on the original site of the 16th-century grammar school founded by Sir John Gresham. Howson began his career at Gresham's here in 1900.

On Sunday, 9th August I saw the first real sign of war. I rode over to Cromer and found a camp of Regulars on the cliffs near the golf links. A curious and rather dramatic event had happened just off the coast that afternoon. A large sailing ship was passing northwards when she was intercepted by a destroyer. She was a German, quite unconscious of the war."

The school chapel in summer 1914. The foundation stone had been laid in 1912.

The remarks of the school doctor, Cassandra-like amid the noisy enthusiasm all around him, are noteworthy. Such voices are not much recorded from the August days of 1914. More characteristic were the persistent, wishful, rumours about a significant naval encounter, echoed in the account in *The Gresham* of the OTC camp held at Tidworth Pennings at the very moment when war was declared:

> "Mention should be made of the wonderful and fearful rumours of great naval victories in the North Sea which were current in the Camp on the last afternoon before England had declared war."

Mention here should also be made of the unfortunate absence from the proceedings of the expected guest of honour who was to have addressed the brigade. Sir Horace Smith-Dorrien was "at the last moment prevented" from attendance, thereby missing the "great patriotic enthusiasm" of the sing-songs. One assumes that as one of the generals commanding the BEF with Haig, he had more pressing business, and indeed he was in France by 7 August, but the writer

The school chapel after its completion.

of the article in *The Gresham* is merely aggrieved that on the Tuesday the camp was:

> "...prematurely dispersed owing to mobilisation. It was most unfortunate that the Brigade field operations arranged for Tuesday and Wednesday should have thus fallen through, as these are always the most interesting part of the Camp work."

Unfortunate indeed. The boy's-eye view was a little different. A young Raymond Berridge was suitably in awe of developments in late July 1914. On the 31st, he wrote from Tidworth Pennings to his mother:

> "Very many thanks for the fruit-cake; it is nicer than ever before. How very serious the war outlook is!"

Ten former Gresham's boys were listed in October 1914 as being in the BEF in France and the first casualties were not slow in coming. Henry Chapman was

Gresham's OTC at Windsor in 1911. Sergeant Steer is in the foreground, second left.

wounded at the Battle of the Marne on 8 September and invalided home. Chapman had received his commission in the Royal Field Artillery in July 1913. At the outbreak of war he went with his battery to France and was, perhaps, one of the first British soldiers to get into close contact with the enemy as, at the Battle of Mons, on Sunday, 23 August, he was sent to take up a position in advance of the infantry. This was an error, and caused Chapman a good deal of difficulty, but in the event he was mentioned in despatches for saving his guns in the retreat from Mons, despite being under very heavy fire. Sixteen hundred British soldiers were killed at Mons on the first day, and losses were even worse – 2,600 killed and missing – during the retreat on the second day, when it was realised that 70,000 faced 160,000 German troops. Only three days after this desperately hard battle, the 5th Division was again engaged, this time at the bigger battle of Le Cateau, where casualties were worse than at Mons. This battle was an attempt to deal the Germans a "stopping blow". They were battering their way to Paris and reached a point only 25 miles away. After some hours of fighting the order was given to the exhausted troops to retire, and those guns which, like Chapman's, were well forward with the infantry were very vulnerable to attack. By the end of the day, indeed, 38 guns and nearly 8,000 men were lost. Chapman's luck ran out on the Marne battlefield, in a battle lasting ten days and involving two million men. His letter back to school was as laconic as any sent home during a war in which understatement was the order of the day:

> "We had a rough time at Mons and again at Le Cateau. Our losses in the 5th Division were very heavy – nearly half our officers – and some regiments lost nearly all. We went back nearly to Paris, and it was in the first battle – on the Marne – after we turned round, that I got hit."

The "rough time" at Mons was described in detail in the account of the incident which led to his mention in despatches:

> "In the evening of Sunday, 23 August, he was ordered by his Major to take one of his guns to help defend a trench where the infantry were very hard pushed, but was told not to fire until daylight the next morning. They had many scares all through that night, and owing to burning houses set on fire by the Germans, he was able to watch the enemy entrenching themselves on the heaps of coal refuse outside the collieries. When daylight appeared he commenced shelling their position incessantly.
>
> Our infantry in the trench after suffering great loss were told to withdraw, leaving their wounded and were to be relieved by another battalion, but owing to the sweeping fire of the enemy the relieving party were unable to reach the trench.
>
> Seeing the position was hopeless and that nearly half his men were wounded, he tried to save his gun; he and his men managed to extricate it by hand to a building in the rear where the horses were sheltered. The difficulty was to get the gun from there, over a space swept by shrapnel and shell fire; so he went by himself to explore the ground and find where the gun could be got through. Having found that there was only one way open and that it was for 100 or 150 yards in full view of the enemy, he ordered the only four horses he had should be hitched on to the gun, and told the two drivers, who have since been mentioned in despatches for this feat, to gallop as hard as they could to the rear and they escaped without hurt or damage to the gun.

He himself had to crawl over the same place under a shower of shrapnel and rifle bullets; when he was about halfway progress seemed so slow that he thought he would try to rush it, but immediately he stood up the fire was concentrated on him and he had promptly to lie flat and crawl again until he got back to the lines."

Less than a week after Henry Chapman was injured, Lancelot Aveling was wounded at the Battle of the Aisne on 14 September, while serving with the Connaught Rangers, and found himself in hospital in Versailles. It was at the Battle of the Aisne, from 13-27 September, that trench warfare began as the Germans sought to halt their retreat by digging in behind the River Aisne, full after the recent rains which marked the end of the hot summer. The infantry fought bravely and tenaciously, but the well-entrenched German artillery won the victory. Aveling recovered from his injuries and was back with his regiment in early October, returning to the front line in November. He fought in the First Battle of Ypres, where he was wounded again on the 7th. This was a "Blighty", an injury sufficiently serious to warrant a return home, so after 11 days in hospital in France he was nursed privately, in Kensington. At about this time he was mentioned in despatches for "gallantry at Le Soupir" (in September). Back he went to the Ypres salient and was wounded again on 26 April 1915. This time he did not recover, and died three days later.

In his service record there is a correspondence between his family and the War Office which sheds a little light on his earlier injuries and on the importance of practical matters even at times of grief. Aveling had had to re-equip himself not once but twice but had not had time to submit a claim before his death. The family wanted to make such a claim on his behalf for loss of kit – a tunic, an overcoat, an 1883 sword of Wilkinson pattern, his revolver and two pairs of breeches cut off after his wounds of September and November 1914. Perhaps the nature of his injuries required the scissors to be taken to these garments, but another explanation is possible. John Buchan, in his memoir of the Grenfell twins Francis and Riversdale, quotes from Francis' diary an incident in which Francis was wounded in the leg and taken to a French convent to be nursed. There his breeches were cut off rather than merely removed, to preserve the modesty of his nurse-nuns! Whatever the case with Lancelot Aveling, the War Office duly paid compensation of £25. The telegram sent home to inform his family of his death was of the usual form, the words "Deeply regret to inform you that" pre-printed on the form, and with the unconvincing ending: "Lord Kitchener expresses his sympathy."

The tributes to Lancelot Aveling reveal a gentle, quiet man, an only son whose end was much regretted by those who knew him. A "Chaplain to the Forces" wrote:

> "It was most wonderful to see your son deal with his men. He was so quiet with them and yet he got everything done which had to be done. I could not help noticing the contrast with some of the others. His men were devoted to him. I had a chat with them about him and they said he was a good officer. "He looks after us well, he does.""

John Kempson, the first of the Greshamians to lose his life and the youngest of all the fatalities, was lost with his ship the *Hawke*, an old British cruiser torpedoed by the German submarine U9 in the North Sea between Peterhead and the Naze in October 1914. The *Hawke* had stopped to pick up some mail from a sister ship. In the early months of the war there was little awareness of the threat from the U-boats and there were several catastrophic incidents with great loss of life, that involving the *Hawke* being one of them. Estimates vary of the precise casualty figures, but all agree that there were many drowned. Fewer than 50 survived from a crew of over 500. A local boy, from Sheringham on the North Norfolk coast, it was perhaps that background which gave John Kempson his early love of the sea. He had joined Gresham's as a day-boy in 1909, won a scholarship and boarded in Old School House for a few months and then left school for Osborne and Dartmouth, passing out, 14th on the list, in April 1914. He served first on HMS *Cumberland* then joined HMS *Hawke*, serving as a midshipman. It seems appropriate that the only surviving photograph of him, taken when he was about 13, shows him in uniform. On the day he died he was only 17 years and four months old.

John Kempson, the first Greshamian to lose his life in the war, and the youngest. He was only 17 years and 4 months old when he died. The photograph is taken from the memorial, on vellum, made by Dallas Wynne Willson.

Cuthbert Shaw was the second fatality of 1914, dying on 30 October near Ypres while serving with the Royal Sussex Regiment. After the Battle of the Aisne, both sides sought a gap to the north between the Aisne and the sea which was not entrenched and which could be gained with advantage to outflank the enemy. In the event, as the lines of trenches clawed their way north, this area was reduced, by early October, to a narrow region of Flanders, open, dreary, and muddy countryside. Both Allied and German commanders focused on Ypres, entered by the BEF on 3 October. From the 29th of that month to 15 November, the BEF were defending an area to the south and east of the fine medieval city under almost constant attack from the German 4th Army. On 20 October the German offensive had begun, the Germans with great superiority in numbers. The line was held by the Allies thanks to the skill of their BEF riflemen, steadily firing between 15 and 30 rounds a minute as they had been trained to do, and by cavalrymen fighting with skill and bravery on foot. Cuthbert Shaw was 20 when he died, alongside four fellow officers, in some fierce fighting on the night of 30-31 October. His local newspaper, describing him blandly and impersonally as "a most promising young soldier", suggested in the same article that there was some hope that he had not been killed, as the War Office advice was that he was "wounded and missing". With the harsh gaze of hindsight, the hope seems touchingly naïve. Shaw remained missing forever afterwards, lost without trace in the Flanders mud, one of 24,000 British soldiers killed in the First Battle of Ypres. His name is now commemorated, with almost 55,000 of his comrades from this and subsequent battles for the salient, on the Menin Gate Memorial.

Immediately following the account of Shaw's death in the school magazine was printed a poem by an OG, Arthur Playford. It has debateable literary merit but serves to show the preconceptions about war common to Howson's generation.

The Lion
"The Lion is asleep," they said,
"Tis safe to start on France,
For should the Lion hear our tread
He will not raise his stupid head
To question our advance.
"Through Belgium we will wend our way
She will not dare resist,
If promises will not persuade,
And threatenings leave her unafraid,
We'll try the mailed fist...
The Lion sprang with mighty strength
To where the need was sore,

> And from the corners of the earth
> The Lion's cubs came tearing forth
> To join him in the war.
> And is the British Lion old,
> His sun about to set? -
> Is he feeble as they said?
> Is he dying? – nearly dead?
> *Not yet,* my boy, *not yet!*

Cuthbert Shaw, pictured in the roll of honour in November 1914.

Cecil Graves, the elder brother of Adrian, and later the Joint Director-General of the BBC, was a casualty of another sort in 1914. He had been reported as missing and it was feared that he had been killed, that is until a cheque from him, dated 26 September, arrived at his bankers through Amsterdam! Taken prisoner while serving with the Royal Scots, he wrote:

> "We are slowly and wearily wending our way towards Germany. We have walked steadily since we were captured, a week ago, and we shall not be put in the train until the day after tomorrow. There is not much news I can tell you but such news as I have heard of the regiment since we got cut off from it is bad, as it seems to have been cut up badly... We have been through a good deal and the discomforts of this march have been numerous. Although we are prisoners we have one great consolation and that is that by hanging on as we did for nine hours after the rest of our army had gone back we probably held up the Germans who would have mercilessly shelled their retreat... A German General asked one of our men who we and the Gordons were, and on being told, he said that we had fought simply splendidly... It is a perfect nightmare to look back upon."

At the Battle of Le Cateau, a battalion of Gordon Highlanders had not received the order to retreat and had held their ground, with disastrous consequences.

John Reith, later Lord Reith, Director-General of the BBC, Minister of Transport and Minister of Information in the Second World War, was making his way to France with the 5th Battalion the Cameronians (Scottish Rifles), in late summer 1914. He had not been very happy at Gresham's, being transplanted at the late age of 14 into boarding education, having to try to make his mark in well-established friendship groups and suffering isolation, as he saw it, because of being the only Scot and the only Presbyterian in the school. Yet he wrote back from the war to a headmaster with whom he had crossed swords over his non-attendance at Sunday evening concerts. He had not had the courage to face the formidable figure of Howson with the truth, which was that his Sabbatarianism was the obstacle. Reith's first letter back to school was brief, but full of enthusiasm:

> "We feel proud of being the first Territorial battalion from Scotland to go to France, and there are very few others here. We had a week of travel, and it was extraordinarily hard work for Transport, but still we got through it. I was not in bed for five nights. Now we have had a week in a little village, but tomorrow we move right up."

Christmas 1914 has entered mythology for its truces, the exchanged gifts and shaken hands between opposing soldiers in No Man's Land, the carol singing and the football match. A week before, John Reith returned to his billet to find:

> "... a letter from my old school. It was written longhand by the Headmaster and signed by 11 others as well – masters and boys. 'We are thinking a good deal about you OGs at the Front. And Gresham's School wants you to know that with the enclosed comes, from every member, thoughts and best wishes at Christmas. We are sending a small box of tuck, etc., which we hope will arrive for the New Year. Signed on behalf of the whole school.' Very touching. Every Thursday night there was a service in the chapel [*then in Big School, of course,*] for serving Old Boys, and our names were read out. It was good to know the school had us in mind."

On the 21st he received a parcel from Gresham's containing a mechanical lighter, a letter signed by four masters and six boys and a further promise of the New Year's tuck box. It can only have been a very small consolation for the absence of letters from young ladies which he felt his fellows were receiving in abundance! There were, however, two boxes of chocolates from a Miss Miller, which he seems to have discounted because he had no idea who she was. Perhaps he had forgotten that his housemaster in Bengal Lodge was Mr Miller, and that he had a daughter. The truth will never be known but it seems likely that a very young admirer had remembered him.

The first months of the war had brought serious injury to a number of OGs, but only two fatalities. On a national scale, however, the BEF had been almost completely wiped out in 1914, and it was the task now of the Kitchener volunteers to provide a good army. The pressure was on. In August a minimum height of 5ft 8ins, good health and good teeth were required in a new recruit. By Christmas the height requirement had reduced to 5ft and teeth had merely to be "sufficient".

Exciting Times up in the Trenches

Alec Herron, Howson's house captain in 1911, (seated on Howson's right). On Herron's right is Arthur Estcourt, MC, and at his feet sit a young David Carnegie and a bespectacled Adrian Graves.

MOST of the Gresham's boys who had hurried to enlist in August 1914 served, predictably, in the trenches of the Western Front. Despite the horrors of warfare which early on became apparent to those serving, some of the first accounts sent to the school magazine in the first autumn of the war reveal all the *joie de vivre* of boys on an exciting school trip. "The Blucher on fire was a wonderful sight," commented Frederic Jacques; the trenches were "pretty comfortable" and the

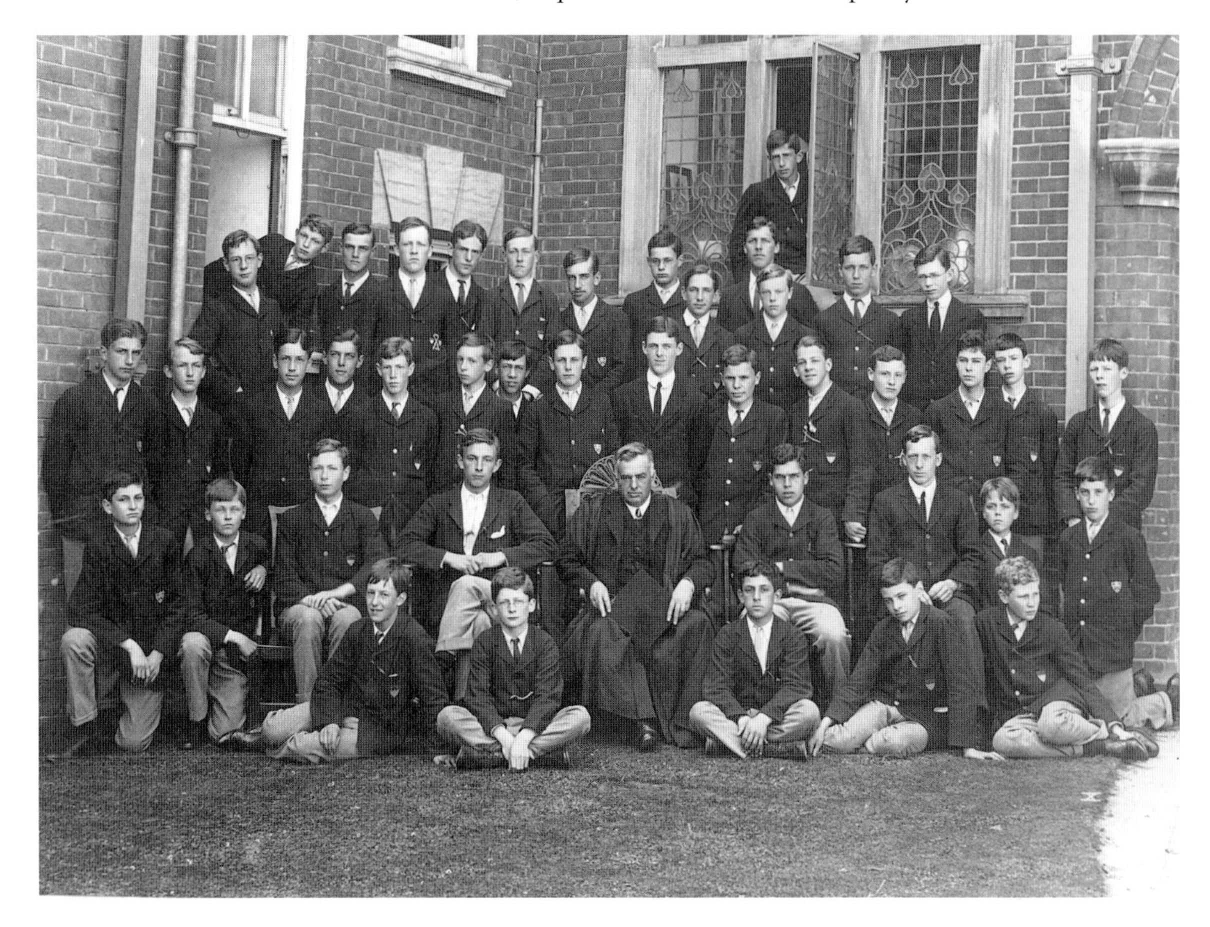

soldiers were "very well fed" remarked a stoical Alec Herron. They were having "exciting times up in the trenches" according to James Foster.

And a small victory was "a beautiful hit the other day" when Charles Springfield managed to destroy a German cookhouse:

> "After the third round I managed to get one right home and into the stew…I am afraid someone went hungry."

Far from the trenches of the Western Front, Geoffrey White, serving with an Australian regiment in Cairo, was particularly enthusiastic. "Very well equipped in every way," and with "the best rifles available", he was more than happy to serve as a private and "awfully proud of being an OG".

Of course, a darker note was struck too. Several of the early letters mention the dreadful weather conditions of France and Belgium and the desperately hard work the men were required to do. Springfield wrote that getting out a bogged down gun "took me 16 hours work in the pouring rain". The elder of the Foster brothers, James, recorded that, "We were knee deep in mud and water while we were in the trenches" in a letter written from his hospital bed.

An exhausted John Middleton recounted one endurance test:

> "We marched all night 20 miles…It was a proper forced march. I had two horses to pull along and all my equipment on. I don't know when I have been so done."

John Reith, having got to the Front, was finding that life was more difficult than perhaps he had expected:

> "One night we were shelled out and I think that is quite the worst thing we have been through. About 800 shells were dropped altogether in the town, and as several fell in among my horses, it was the time to clear out which we did and without loss of a man, horse or waggon…The bombardment lasted from 9.30pm to 6.30am, so at 7 we solemnly returned and resumed where we had left off. They touch us up periodically, but there has been nothing like it since, and I can't pretend to be thirsting for another such night."

One belated but no doubt welcome arrival recorded in the letters of early 1915 was that of "strong rubber top boots". It was not surprising that trench foot was so common. Captain William Holmes wrote in bitterly ironical mood:

> "I am so sorry I never answered your letter, but I was occupied all the time by stemming the advance of 'Modern Kultur' in a somewhat hurried hole in the ground. Of course no one can have an idea what it is like until you have been there. It is merely scientific slaughter, in which, I am glad to say, we can more than hold our own."

Yet the prevailing mood was determinedly cheerful, maybe for the sake of those at home, or maybe because making the best of things was a deeply-ingrained attitude, particularly if one was writing to one's former headmaster. James Foster had suffered badly from the mud and water but said only:

> "The hospital is very fine and comfortable, and when my feet are fit to walk with I shall be back with John [*his brother*] again."

The wet weather, which was causing so much misery in the trenches of Flanders, held up work at Gresham's on the chapel as well. The figures were

The chapel in the spring of 1915.

The chapel interior, also in spring 1915.

indeed remarkable. The rainfall for the Holt area in the winter months is usually about 2-3ins per month: in December 1914 and January 1915 the total was 11.03ins.

At school, games had been relegated to a position of even less importance than hitherto as all attention focused, patriotically, on the Corps. The editor of the school magazine explained this decision in detail:

> "The voluntary abandonment of House Matches [*is*] an indication that the school recognises the relative unimportance of games at a time such as this, and desires, at the same time, to do nothing to impair the solidarity of the School as a whole."

No longer armed with "weapons of precision", the boys were practising on the miniature range and learning about musketry. Corporal Raymond Berridge was proving an effective teacher of signalling, and Sergeant Dawson Atkin, after a

Raymond Berridge in a Woodlands house prefects photograph from 1915.

period of "nocturnal incubation", had brought forth a band which helped keep the marching in step. Boys will be boys, however, and teachers ever teachers:

> "It is with diffidence that we use the pages of *The Gresham* to suggest that it is characteristic of the good soldier to be proud of his uniform and to wear it with a feeling that it confers on him an obligation to adorn it. We may be straining after gnats when we insist that attempts to improve His Majesty's uniform by adding a bilious yellow scarf are unnecessary; that both lack of, and too much attention to, the hair is unsoldierly; and that shoulder blades that might interest an anatomist are viewed by the soldier with abhorrence..."

Despite the humour, it is clear that valuable training was being undertaken and that at least some of the boys approached it in a spirit of enthusiasm.

The school was faced with one or two privations, of course, but the admirable response of those in the trenches was not always replicated there. On 27 January 1915, Daylight Saving Time was introduced to Gresham's because the police were concerned that the school, brightly lit between 5pm and 6 pm, would be a good target for Zeppelins. This entailed schoolboys having to get up not only an hour earlier, but an hour earlier than *everyone else*! This, unsurprisingly, did not win favour with the "weaker brethren".

However, the fears of a Zeppelin attack on the school were justified in January 1915, as by the 27th of that month there had already been a raid. Two Zeppelins, the L3 and the L4, trying to find the Humber, lost their course in the wintry conditions of the night of 19 January and in the fog and rain, both made landfall in Norfolk. The first, the L3, dropped the first bombs ever to fall from the sky on English soil, on Great Yarmouth. The raid lasted ten minutes, killing two people

Dawson Atkin (standing third from right, back row) in the rugby team of 1913. George Fenchelle (holding the ball), Denys Rogers (seated on the ground at Fenchelle's feet), David Carnegie (seated to Rogers' left) and Adrian Graves (back row extreme left) also lost their lives in the war.

and injuring three others. The L4 crossed the coastline over Bacton and passed Cromer. At Sheringham the pilot tried to find out where he was, looming below the cloud cover at only about 800ft, his face clearly visible to surprised watchers in the High Street. Wynne Willson recalled:

> "We were among the first people to see or hear them when they came over England. We were told at Holt that a Zeppelin was hovering over Sheringham; they had a 4.7 gun on the links there, but I believe its elevation was not great enough and its use would have meant considerable retaliation on the town. As it was, they dropped two or three small bombs, which were the first actually dropped on English soil. At about eight o'clock they came over us at Holt, and we put out all lights. The little boys in my boarding house were on the whole more excited than alarmed. [*Wynne Willson's son, Bill, then a child of three and a half, remembered, 85 years later, being brought downstairs for safety when the Zeppelins*

> *came over.*] Luckily for the inhabitants of the boarding house, the bombs all fell round a farmhouse, killing one or two sheep and a turkey, and dislodging some tiles. Next day the school repaired thither en masse to inspect the damage and the boys searched the small craters for bits of bombs; they collected from round the farm quite a large store of old scrap iron which had probably lain there for decades. I remember taking a parcel of sweets down for the small children at the farmhouse, who had of course been very much frightened."

So had one or two of Wynne Willson's young charges. In the words of Wynne Willson's daughter, then aged six:

> "Two boys where going home when they heard a bomb 100 yards away they turned round and they threw there bykes into the hedge and bolted to the Old School House they where very fritened several boys where crying."

One young member of Old School House at the time was Geoffrey Diggle, who was not so much frightened by the Zeppelins as disappointed that they had not caused more dramatic damage. In his old age, he recalled that all that appeared were "six small craters in a turnip field". He also recounted that at evening prayers the boys sang a hymn, the housemaster sometimes:

> "…when we were in full flow, putting in a bit of tenor. His final prayer concluded: 'Lord grant us a quiet night and a perfect end' – some of us thought that this referred to the Zeppelins."

Holt and Sheringham had been lucky, King's Lynn less so. There the L4 dropped more bombs, killing a woman and a small boy and injuring 13 others. This attack on 19 January caused, as might be imagined, a great sensation in Norfolk. For the first time, civilian casualties had come to Britain, and Norfolk was seeing the agents of death *first*. The stalwart Norfolk inhabitants did not panic, although the raids made a great impression. Even the *Norfolk Chronicle*, whose coverage of the war at this point generally began on page six, well behind the regular articles on seasonal fruit, the diseases of vegetables, and local gentry marriages, led on the Friday following with an article on the Zeppelin raid.

The first Greshamian to die in 1915 was not killed by the enemy but was a victim of septicaemia. Frederick Spurrell died in Brighton after a long fight against the infection of a gunshot wound to his left hand. He had spent 18 days in hospital before being discharged to duty, returning to hospital again two weeks later with an unhealed and festering wound. He died three days later.

Across the Channel in the spring of 1915, the trenches of the Western Front were becoming more elaborate. They were still prone to flooding in low-lying areas, and they were scarcely comfortable, but generally speaking they were more solid and habitable than before. Defended now by barbed wire entanglements, and equipped with dugouts and a system of support and reserve trenches to the rear, these were far more substantial constructions than the rough-and-ready, hastily scraped out waist-high British trenches of the First Battle of Ypres. The most vivid description of these early trenches by a Greshamian came from Willoughby Chapman, the elder brother of Henry:

> "I envy some fellows their trenches! I wish ours were anything like them. The last ones I came out of the other day were 25 yards from the Germans; the parapet was not as high as my waist and not bullet proof at the top. We had no loopholes – they were shot away as soon as we put them up – at least sandbags were and others were not safe to use as they shot through them, and they kept potting the whole time. We could not answer them as the loopholes in their parapet were right low down, so that our fellows were against the sky if they fired over the parapet at them… The mud in my trench was only about 6ins to 1ft deep, but there was a lot of blood and sundry corpses in it, and one had to crawl along it to avoid showing over the parapet. That is the worst trench I have been in for danger and anxiety, I think; it was taken and retaken only the other day, and one was on tenter-hooks the whole time, as, if they did come, they would be on us before one knew much about it, and we had no wire in front of us… The Germans had one sap to within 15 yards of where I was sitting."

We Do Not Forget

DESPITE descriptive accounts of trench life and the battlefields by OGs, even in April 1915 the reality of war had still not fully come home to those at school in North Norfolk. Censorship and the policy of local newspapers to keep local news to the fore meant that there was little media information for many people in England. The editor of *The Gresham* confessed that it was "almost impossible for us to gain any conception of what modern war is really like". The paradox was of a war which was physically quite close – it was said that the sound of the guns could be heard by Gresham's boys huddled under a nearby railway bridge – yet the imagination could not grasp the actuality of the detail.

In practical terms, the non-arrival of stone for the chapel was "one of the very few ways in which the war has adversely affected the progress of the building operations" and one suspects one of the few ways in which the war in early 1915 made a direct impact on the school, at a distance from the town, at all. A shortage of men at the quarries and problems with a railway system whose first call was from the government accounted for the delays.

For the most part, rightly, the life of the school continued as usual. A violin and pianoforte recital, the acquisition of a new section of books on modern languages for the library, the shooting, all testify to business as usual, although the debating topic for the Lent Term was topical. "This House would regret the adoption in England of compulsory military service." It certainly would, as the motion was carried by 43 votes to five. In this respect the debaters of Gresham's echoed precisely the national view. The voting figures suggest a well-attended meeting: the remarks of 21 speakers were recorded, four of whom are familiar from the list of the fallen.

As to the important matter of food, at that stage of the war Greshamians continued to do pretty well. Breakfast was porridge, sometimes, inevitably, lumpy; bread, butter and eggs. Lunch was meat and two vegetables, a traditional steamed pudding or rhubarb, and tea consisted of bread and butter with extras provided by the boys themselves. Geoffrey Diggle remarked that a small pot of Golden Syrup was only 4d at that time.

Although the war seemed far away, the casualty lists were growing, and bad news began filtering through. Alec Herron was killed in action at Neuve Chapelle, 20 miles south of Ypres, serving as a second-lieutenant with the King's Royal Rifle

Corps, on 10 March 1915. His was only the fourth death suffered by the school, and the shock of losing such a "golden lad" was profound. The action on the day he died consisted of an attack on the ruined village of Neuve Chapelle, which, it was expected, would take the Germans completely by surprise. It was part of a major allied offensive, but at the time British troops were being moved from the area to go to Gallipoli. The heavy bombardment by 342 guns, begun at 7.30 in the morning, was unprecedented in its intensity and severity. Denis Winter, in *Death's Men,* comments that more shells were fired at Neuve Chapelle in that 35-minute period than in the whole of the Boer War. The village was taken quite easily, but it proved difficult to push forward to the Aubers Ridge, as had been planned, and the Allied advance was only about one to two kilometres.

Alec Herron in uniform pictured in the roll of honour 1915.

Herron was one of a total of nearly 13,000 casualties on that day, but to Gresham's he was very much more than a bare statistic. Described as a "boy of brilliant all-round abilities", Alec (or Alick, as his name was spelt on his birth certificate and in the school register) had been captain of the headmaster's house, and captain of the school. So able that he had been promoted to the sixth form when aged only 14, he had won a history scholarship to New College, Oxford, and had gained a first-class degree in July 1914. It was thus only months before his death that the school had congratulated him heartily on this achievement. His housemaster in the Junior School at Gresham's, Dallas Wynne Willson, spoke of him thus, bracketing him with Adrian Graves:

> "...it seemed as though the war took the cream. Early in the war [*not in fact an accurate memory – Graves was killed in 1918*] two brilliant boys were killed, Alec Herron, Scholar of New College, and Adrian Graves, son of C. L. Graves of *The Spectator* and brother of Sir Cecil Graves of the BBC. A year or so before I had had to teach these two boys Greek as Greek was then required to enter Oxford and was not taught at Gresham's. I never in all my scholastic experience met any boys who galloped through Greek grammar as these two did. They simply lapped it up."

It is not surprising that another school source should comment on Herron's "sterling qualities, his high sense of honour, his generosity and his winning personality", but the letters sent to his parents after his death also reveal an exceptional response to the young man. His commanding officer wrote to Herron's father:

> "Dear Mr Herron,
> I am very sorry indeed that I have very bad news to give you. The Battalion attacked the German trenches on the 10th inst., and there were many casualties, and among them your son. He was leading his men most gallantly, and was shot when quite close to the German trenches. It has not been possible to recover his body, as the trenches were not captured, but I fear that I can hold out no hope whatever that he has not been killed, as a sergeant and three men, who escaped, are all absolutely certain that your son was dead... He led his men magnificently, and everyone speaks of him with the greatest praise. I very much fear that there will be no possibility of recovering his body until the German trenches are captured as it is lying just by the wire entanglement of the German trench. All those who saw him assure me that he was killed at once, so I hope he did not suffer."

That letter, although sincere, seems less significant than the one sent to the *Liverpool Echo* by Rifleman Charles Miles:

> "I should be very pleased if you could find a small space in your valuable paper in regard to the brave officer who led us in our charge on the morning of 10 March.
>
> We had to cover 250 yards of heavy ground. Our officer got to within five yards of the German trench when he was shot down. He had not time to recover himself when he was hit a second time, and this killed a brave fellow.
>
> The gentleman I refer to is 2nd Lieutenant Herron of Liverpool. I shall never forget him. He was such a good fellow to all of us. I am sure all of us feel his loss. He died like a soldier and a man."

Deference and admiration are distancing emotions, but here there is warmth and fellowship too. Charles Miles shows no sign of a divide in sympathies between officers and men who served together in the trenches. It would be wrong to speak of camaraderie where there was not personal friendship, but the fumbling words of the letter, and the very act of writing it, bespeak the great respect and liking in which Herron was held.

Another wartime colleague wrote:

> "I have only been with the company about two months, but in that time I found out what sterling qualities your boy had. He was always most painstaking and hardworking and always had his platoon in most excellent order... It was practically a new Company only formed about four months ago, and they have done as well as the best seasoned troops could have done. Everyone says they were simply magnificent."

A school friend spoke of:

> "his conscientiousness and high ideals. We always knew that he was
> One who never turned his back but marched breast forward,
> Held we fall to rise, are baffled to fight better,
> Sleep to wake."

The lines are taken from Robert Browning's *Epilogue,* which has traditionally closed all editions of Browning's poetry, and they are lines referring to Browning himself. The poet was inclined at one point to withdraw them as being "bragging", but wrote, "it's the simple truth; and as it's true it shall stand." For Browning, bravery was a highly regarded quality, and it is interesting that these same lines, more fully quoted, were applied to Howson in the editorial in *The Gresham* published after his death in 1919.

Despite the expressed hopes of his commanding officer, Alec Herron's body was never recovered. He is commemorated today on the Le Touret Memorial, near Bethune.

Letters of sympathy and tributes from officers and friends are sometimes a valuable source of information about those who fell in the war, but they can be disappointingly impersonal. Most commanding officers usually carried out their unenviable task to the best of their ability, although there are plenty of signs that sometimes, as the war went on, perhaps because of sheer weight of numbers or lack of personal knowledge of a man only newly arrived in their company, they resorted to comforting clichés or a set formula. Those OGs who speak through their *own* letters undoubtedly emerge the most vividly, and, perhaps because of the bond between them and their former headmaster, Gresham's boys wrote back more often to school than most. Letters to a headmaster must have certain characteristics. On the one hand the writers could be more honest about conditions than they would wish to be in letters to anxious parents. On the other, they would convey the values the headmaster had espoused and taught. It is not likely that a young man writing back to an idealistic and perhaps idealised schoolmaster would express fear, or complain of his lot. He would write what his former teacher wanted to hear. There are thus benefits and disadvantages in such a correspondence. One definite gain is that the boys seem to have relished the opportunity provided by war for a reversal of roles. In these circumstances the taught became the teachers. Howson could tell them nothing about modern warfare – they could decide exactly what they told him. Alec Herron is best known to us by his letters to school, and the self he projected was resolute, proud of his company, enthusiastic. This is not to suggest that these were not truths about himself, but only that much must have been excluded.

The second of his three letters back to school is the stuff of which history books are made. Detailed, articulate and atmospheric, it tells of life in the trenches of Ypres in the autumn of 1914:

> "We were in the trenches three days in all, and were, everything considered pretty comfortable. We had a little snow, very little, but no rain, and our trenches were dry, being situated on a high brickfield on a ridge. The soil was strong and so did not cave in easily, even with frost, and we had plenty of brick to make a floor. You know trenches in loose soil, potato fields and the like, are very apt to cave in and in low ground they fill with water and it is impossible to drain them unless one is in a lucky spot. There is one spot near here known as 'Bloody Corner', a salient on low ground where the water is everywhere over the knees. We met some of the Royal Sussex, who had just come out of them. Cold feet is, of course, a universal evil in trenches at this time of year. We had braziers to get them warm at, but not nearly enough fuel; indeed there was only enough for the men to cook their food at. The worst of it is that it prevents one sleeping when one has a chance. One is very well fed, getting Machonachie rations each day; one simply heats the tin for a few minutes and there is a hot vegetable and meat stew before one, but as officers found, our minds were so occupied that we did not want much to eat. We were busy all day getting the trench deepened and so on, and at night we took relief, six hours on, six hours off, but we often missed part of our six hours, too cold

to sleep, or because we feared an attack and thought we must be ready. Then remaking loopholes blown to bits by their snipers was always a business, and we had continually to be keeping the men cleaning their rifles, as mud and dirt getting into the bolts clog them and make them useless. So that when we did get out we were really pretty tired, though we had not felt it much while we were there. After two nights' rest I feel as fit as a fiddle, and I have not a trace of a cold. Their snipers were very good indeed, and our loopholes were very worn, but as they were so close we had to keep the men looking out the whole time. Probably if they had rushed us at night we would have got very few shots in, and the first thing we would have known would have been the Germans leaping into our trenches. So we had bayonets fixed all the time. The company on our right have much better trenches, and as the Germans were 800 yards off they put up targets and signalled bulls or misses. Past them are the French and they are a fine lot. One of their machine-gun officers came over to see our lines and I had to conduct him back to make sure he was not a spy. They had very comfortable trenches and it is rather stirring to see their sentries hooded and standing up as still as lamp posts."

Herron's last letter to Gresham's, printed in the school magazine, is but three columns away from the account of his death:

"We are on one of the few pieces of high ground in the country, and consequently our trenches are fairly dry, which is one of the greatest blessings troops can have out here. The Adjutant has been adding up the number of men who have been sent home sick in the battalion since the war started. We have a splendid record. Since the war began about 2,500 men have been with the battalion. There have been about 1,500 casualties – killed, wounded and sick sent to hospital. The sick only amount to 120 in seven months, that is 5 per cent for the whole period, and well under 1 per cent per month. The figures for the whole division are so low that the Headquarters Staff would not believe them at first."

Every death is equally important, every loss a special loss to those who knew the young man who fell. So many years on, the record does not allow equal attention to each one of the fallen of Gresham's. Many of the army records of

Marlborough Crosse (left) and his younger brother Ewins Crosse who died within two months of one another in the spring of 1915.

those who served in the ranks, for example, were burnt in German bombing in the Second World War and simply destroyed. There are some lives and deaths, though, which through the survival of personal accounts such as those of Alec Herron or through the particularly sad details attached to them, affect the reader more directly than others. One such was the story of the Crosse brothers, Marlborough and Ewins.

Marlborough, the elder, was known to his friends at school as "Ugly", a nickname he seems to have been happy to accept perhaps because he knew perfectly well that it was not an accurate description. Surviving photographs, one particularly striking, in theatre costume, show a strapping young man – 5ft 10ins tall and broad-chested according to his medical form – with dark rugged features far from ugly, but different from the more smooth-faced, boyish looks of many of his contemporaries. His school obituary speaks of " a singing voice which was, to say the least of it, remarkable. A fully-developed voice of such power and range is rarely, if ever, heard at an early age. He recognised it as a gift and devoted it unsparingly to the service of our School music." He was a close friend of Geoffrey Johnson, another fine school musician, who was killed in action in November 1915. Both were in Bengal Lodge, Johnson the house captain, Crosse a school prefect, and they must have worked closely together in these roles as well as in class. A happy photograph shows the two of them at OTC camp in 1912. Marlborough was serving with the 2nd Yorkshires, the Green Howards, in autumn 1914, and to his great excitement he was given charge of a company of regulars. He wrote:

> "I have been back two days from the trenches which I enjoyed immensely. "The German snipers are awful. Put your hand over the parapet of the trench and you find yourself with a finger missing."

He was right. The German snipers were very accurate. They received special training and always stayed on the same section of the Front, so that they became familiar with it in the greatest detail. In February 1915, Crosse was given the task of drawing a plan of the battlefield:

> "...and of course, every time I put my head over the parapet – crash – and over came a bullet. They followed me all along the trenches. Every time I bobbed up they spotted me. In one place in front of us they have had the cheek to dig (during the night) an advanced trench – only about a 100 yards long and only about 100 yards away from our own front! We shall soon be shaking hands! I expect we shall have some nasty work with the bayonet one dark night!"

But that was not to be. One month later the snipers found their target. On 13 March 1915, Marlborough was killed at Neuve Chapelle, only three days after Herron, while trying to mend one of his machine-guns. "Just as he had finished, a bullet took him through the temple. He died instantly."

His commanding officer wrote to his mother, as his father was in India working as an inspector of schools. "He was buried where he fell. His brother came here yesterday and heard the sad news." Ewins Crosse then returned to his regiment, the Leicesters. On 16 May, only two months after his brother's death, he was mortally wounded while leading his men in an attack on a German trench. This time there was no small comfort for his parents in the belief that their second son's death was "instantaneous". In a letter remarkable for its painful honesty, Ewins Crosse's CO wrote of the 19-year-old boy:

> "He lay where he fell, within 20 yards of the entrenched Germans all night, mostly unconscious, watched over by one of his men, and died the next day."

There survives a photograph of Marlborough Crosse at the age of 20, on his way to Cambridge just one year before he died. On the back of it is written his

Charlie Kirch, acting captain in the Bedfordshire Regiment at the age of 20, the circumstances of whose death remain a mystery.

mother's tribute. "Our hero boy, who died in early years, In men's regret he lives, in women's tears."

Charlie Kirch was one of those commended by his former headmaster, in that he had hurried to attest on 6 August 1914, becoming a private in the Artists' Rifles. The following year he joined the Bedfordshire Regiment and was killed on 19 April 1915 at Hill 60, near Ypres, while acting as captain of his company. The pathos of Kirch's story lies in its unrevealed quality. His only tribute in the school magazine was a brief extract from his major's letter, complimentary but conventional. "He did not know what fear or danger was." At first the details of his death were shrouded in mystery, not even his mother knowing what had happened to him. Her home was in New South Wales, Australia, and all her correspondence was through her London bank, a fact which lends a particularly impersonal air to a story which throughout seems bare-boned. By 8 May the only information received, from the field service base, was that he had died "in the field", and that his place of burial was not known. The War Office declared as late as 21 May only that he had been killed in action "in North West Europe, the exact place not being stated".

At last, on 28 June, after what must have been a very distressing wait, Mrs Kirch was informed that her son had been buried in the grounds of Ypres Asylum, (what grim resonance might that have held for her?) although later his remains were reburied in a war cemetery. The slight scraps of this story of a young man's life and death are echoed in the last details of it. The only personal effects returned to his mother were his wristwatch and strap – fashionable in 1915, as a fobwatch would have been more usual – and a diary. His estate also went to his mother, in the small sum of £90 8s 10d.

By June of 1915 the mood of those at the Front was more sombre, as the casualty list of their friends grew. Five deaths were reported in *The Gresham* of that month, and six men were recorded as having been wounded. One young man met his death, not at the hands of the enemy, but by accident. Hedley Knowles, of the 6th Battalion Duke of Wellington's West Riding Regiment, was killed by a rifle grenade which exploded while he and some fellow soldiers were experimenting with a stand they had invented. The Skipton local newspaper was at pains to "set at rest any idea that might have been entertained that the young

Hedley Knowles, (left) the first officer from the town of Skipton to die in the war, in May 1915. He belonged to the Duke of Wellington's West Riding Regiment as did another Gresham's man from Skipton, Norman Procter MC, (right) who died in 1918.

officer was in any way guilty of carelessness in his performance of duty". The cause was "a mechanical defect" in the grenade, and indeed, "the Grenade Company behaved splendidly at the funeral". Hedley Knowles' parents, of course, grieved deeply for their only son, but their shock was also echoed by the local community. Knowles was the first officer from Skipton to die, and the loss of this dutiful, "gentle and unassuming" 22-year-old law student meant that his Yorkshire community would "have to prepare with stiffened courage" for all that would follow. The conduct of soldiers still evoked the images of sport:

> "With the rod, the gun or the golf club, he ever played the game for the game's sake, just as he played his country's game for his country's sake."

The editor of the school magazine was even now experiencing the same struggle to understand the brutality of war. He commented that "never has... this part of the country where the School lies appeared more beautiful than it does this Spring". As the reality and unreality of war jostled for supremacy he wrote:

> "We cannot help being struck by the force of the contrast between the peaceful loveliness of this quiet countryside and the horrors of the battlefields of Flanders. It seems almost an incongruity that Nature should continue to deck herself in her best during such a calamity."

Yet the familiarity and constancy of the beautiful Norfolk countryside seems to have comforted the editor in the face of unnamed "horrors". In fact, the new horror at Ypres in the spring of 1915 was chlorine gas.

Gradually the magazine reflected the impact of the war. More and more of the text was devoted to letters from the men at the Front. A long article entitled "Mothers and Sons" was reprinted from *The Times.* It had had been inspired by the death of Alec Herron and the writer, an Oxford contemporary of Herron, quoted from *Ecclesiastes,* from the fourth act of Shakespeare's *Cymbeline,* and finally used Ben Jonson's lines to find meaning in the deaths of the young.

> "It is not growing like a tree
> In bulk, doth make man better be.
> In small proportions we just beauties see;
> And in small measures life may perfect be."

In the same edition, an account was given of the decision of Howson and the Gresham's teaching staff to create a war memorial in the school chapel in the form of the organ screen, panelling and stalls, the total cost of which was estimated at £1,003. The cost of a stall and front in English oak "entirely worked by hand" was estimated at that time to be £20. Subscriptions were proving:

> "…few and far between during the last few months, but there is one type of donation to the Chapel Fund that is peculiar to the war and deserves special mention. We refer to the cheques received during the last few months from Old Boys who are serving, whether at home or at the Front; several of these cheques have come straight from the trenches."

Touchingly, Herron's family had donated the £70 due to his estate at the time of his death, Frederick Spurrell's parents gave £20 in memory of their son, and Howson and Eccles gave £100 and £50 respectively.

The editor, meanwhile, persisted in his optimism – "Let us hope that this hurricane will soon pass, leaving the world a sweeter, fresher place" – but there was little sweet or fresh for those in the trenches in April and May of 1915. Guy

Tyler, serving with the 1st Battalion of the Norfolk Regiment, wrote from Hill 60 during the Second Battle of Ypres:

> "We have now been in the firing line and close support for three weeks during which time I have, of course, been out of doors all the time – up in the morning always by 3 o'clock, often not sleeping at night at all, but in the comparative safety of daytime. No bath and my clothes never off, this is what I feel more than anything."

His anger showed too in the same letter:

> "The feeling of all of us here is that the workmen in England should be put under military law... if the supply of munitions suddenly gives out, they simply leave the men to be slaughtered, in just as definite a way as if a sentry goes to sleep on his post."

Arnold Barker, a native of Sunderland, serving, like three more of his brothers, with the Durham Light Infantry, echoed Tyler's physical discomforts. He commented that "home" was a dugout "about one-fifth of my study at school" (in Woodlands), and that his idea of luxury there fell "far short of anything more than a wash, a good feed of bread and eggs, and a nice hayloft to sleep in".

Claude Rouse, a contemporary of Geoffrey Johnson and Henry Russell, would have welcomed some fresh food too, as he hated "bully beef and biscuits", but for him there was a worse irritant. "The mosquitoes are making themselves an awful nuisance – one wakes up in the morning covered with bites."

For several of the men the main subject was danger rather than discomfort. One local young man from Sheringham, Eric Hirtzel, who fought in the Second Battle of Ypres, wrote of "the awful mechanical throb breaking the stillness of the night" being "very unnerving and the bullets only two feet or so above our heads." Worse was to come. In a second letter he spoke vividly and in harrowing terms of a disastrous attack:

> "We made an attack after bombarding after three quarters of an hour and failed miserably. The effect was the same as if we had had no bombardment, whole companies mowed down 15 yards beyond our trenches."

In a later letter, Hirtzel described the bizarre contrasts of war:

> "Two gas shells came over and we put on our masks; such a lovely day too, it seemed ridiculous to have our mouths covered with pieces of flannel."

The attack that followed he remarked:

> "was slaughter pure and simple... One man had his face blown in, but stumbled along towards the dressing station. I put a back for him and ran with him to the station, and came back, but was streaming with the poor fellow's blood."

Occasionally, beauty emerged in the midst of hell. This was the theme of a letter from Kenneth Lloyd of the London Regiment:

> "It was a perfectly calm night and, while we were resting behind the hill, the men lit candles, of which there had just been a very lavish issue. Afterwards when we moved off, as it was so screened from sight and the night so calm, they still carried their candles and from the rear of the battalion we could see them winding in and out among the lanes, which were very intricate. It looked like some wonderful pilgrim's progress, and the windings of the road made the lights cross and recross each other and pass in a most picturesque way."

George Hawksley, of Cromer, was serving at Richebourg near Neuve Chapelle in the Inniskilling Fusiliers. A vivid account of an attack at five in the morning, with the customary *sang froid* of the First World War soldier, conveys every stage of the events, the waiting, the mistakes, the waterlogged trenches, the whizzing bullets:

> "I heard that over half our officers had been knocked over, and later I found that I was the only officer to come back from this trench unhurt."

Later, however, when he could allow himself the luxury of writing at greater length, Hawksley described warmly the assault of the Highland regiments, the Black Watch and the Camerons. "At a loping trot and with their pipes skirling" they went on "though they dropped right and left" and reached the German trench. Once there the achievement was nugatory, as they could not get any further and were ordered back:

George Hawksley from Cromer, whose experiences, described powerfully in his letters, took their toll of his health.

> "Only about a quarter of those who went out came back... Then, tired as they were, they were out in front all night fetching in their wounded and refused all offers of being relieved while a single 'Jock' was out there; one man actually rescued a badly wounded officer from the German parapet itself, and saw the enemy repairing the trenches almost within touching distance."

Hawksley spoke bravely, but it is perhaps significant that in the following June he was admitted to hospital in Fulham suffering from "debility". The strain of battle, even for him, was not ultimately to be denied.

For the first time in the spring months of 1915, the letters from the Western Front began to reveal the unspeakable aspects of war and the effects of such trauma. The desire to keep a strict self-control and to spare those at home the horrors in graphic detail were much to the fore, but the continuing slaughter was too much to be borne.

Nineteen-year-old George Brown, native of the pretty Norfolk village of Attleborough, was contemplating with dread the nightmare of returning to Hill 60, in an area where 168 tons of chlorine gas had been discharged by the Germans over a four-mile front on 22 April:

> "We finish our so-called rest today and move again tonight. I hope it is not to the Hill again as the memories associated with it are too awful. I daresay you have read about the railway cutting which runs from just past Zillebeke Station through the Hill. Well, if ever there was a hell on earth it is in that cutting, full of dead and dying as it was... Almost worse than the wounded are the men who have been gassed, as in most cases they are absolutely helpless. One died practically as I was helping him along; two others I found who had crawled into dugouts to die... I can quite imagine a man's nerves going at a time like this, in fact our own are not what they were since our gruelling."

In his account of the First World War, John Keegan says of this spot: "Today the pockmarks of this tiny battlezone still exude an atmosphere of morbidity sinister even among the relics of the Western Front."

But it was not only France that saw atrocities in the spring of 1915. The Gallipoli campaign, which began in April, became notorious for military misjudgement, for appalling conditions and terrible losses provoking heartfelt revulsion. Winston Churchill, at that time in command of the Royal Navy, believed that an attack on Turkey would help the Allied war effort, because if the Turks were knocked out of the war, then vital supplies could be taken to Russia across the Black Sea, through the Dardanelles Straits. The idea had theoretical merit. Unfortunately, the attack was well known in advance, and the Turks were waiting for the British and ANZAC troops who arrived there in April 1915. From the beginning, Allied casualties were heavy, as the Turks fired upon their armies from the surrounding easily-defended scrubby high land. Geoffrey White, a private in the Australian Mediterranean Expeditionary Force, was in the first boat of the first landing party of the Australian Infantry at Anzac Cove on 25 April. An anonymous friend and fellow Greshamian provides a vivid account of events on that day published in *The Gresham*:

> "Wounded in the leg he still carried on and not until his right arm was damaged by shrapnel did he fall out of the actual fighting line. He was still able to walk and had the use of his left arm, so devoted his energy to supplying ammunition. On his last journey back he came upon a man with half his foot blown off, so, throwing him on his shoulder, he carried him back to the hospital, a distance of two miles. He was so exhausted then by his great efforts and wounds that the Red Cross people would not let him return, but put him in the transport with the other wounded."

White was invalided to Egypt whence he wrote at the end of a controlled and factual letter:

> "It seems unhealthy to fall wounded into the Turks' hands. We had too many wounded to deal with and some rotten things happened, too beastly to talk about. I must stop, my arm gets tired easily. I ought to be back in a little over a fortnight."

Back he went indeed, to rejoin the Allied troops still trapped between cliffs and

sea, but was killed in action on 28 June, about two months later, aged 22.

In the summer of 1915, *The Gresham* transcribed an interview given by the Foster brothers, John and James, to the *Sunderland Echo*. It described events at Aubers Ridge, beyond Neuve Chapelle, where George Goodall had died on 9 May of that year – the disastrous failure to take the German trenches, and the huge casualties. Goodall was a second-lieutenant with the East Lancashire Regiment, whose official history gives details of the action. From the beginning it was thought doubtful that the plan to take the ridge would succeed, as the Germans were aware of the coming offensive and shelled the British trenches systematically. Furthermore, the British lines were in full view of the enemy. The British bombardment began, nonetheless, at 5am on 9 May, and seemed a great success, although it had in fact been ineffective. The men who moved forward were met by continuous rifle and machine-gun fire. At 1pm the British bombardment began again, but this time the shrapnel was hitting the British soldiers themselves. At the end of the "most disastrous day, with one possible exception, that the battalion experienced during the war", the casualties were ten officers killed, including Goodall, with a further nine wounded, 63 other ranks killed, 325 wounded and 42 men missing.

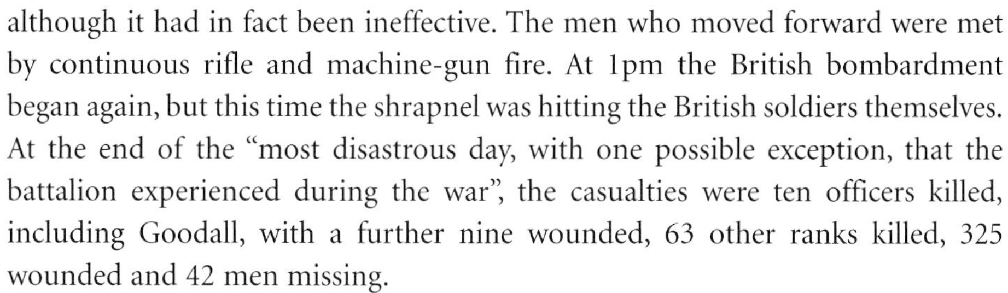

George Goodall, pictured in the roll of honour 1915. His hasty wartime marriage was perhaps not all it seemed.

Although aged only 21, George Goodall had married at the beginning of March, in Plymouth, and a few days later had begun his active service in France. There were many such hasty wartime marriages of course, but Goodall's service record reveals more detail about the circumstances of his. The first unusual feature of the record is a pencilled remark next to the typed note naming his father his next-of-kin. The words read: "Wait. There's a widow." The widow, Dorothy Goodall, claimed, naturally enough, a widow's pension, citing two reputable men in her local community – a retired rear-admiral and a retired chaplain – to stand as character witnesses supporting the rightness of her claim. But almost at once the Army Council was made aware of a possible problem by Goodall's family, who suggested that the police should be asked about the young Mrs Goodall's character. Goodall's parents had, it seems, known nothing of the young woman until after their son had married her. Meanwhile, Dorothy herself was writing in desperate terms begging for financial support – "I am *absolutely* pennyless and destitute" – enclosing the last letter she had received from George Goodall, which, she claimed, showed his enduring love for her. She hoped for an £80 annual pension and £100 gratuity for his death in action. But the police report was damning:

> "I am informed from a very reliable source that for several years previous to her marriage she led an immoral life. She met her husband through his being billeted with her sister a short distance from this town. For a few days after her marriage, during the time that her husband remained here, her conduct was satisfactory. After he had left for the Front she led a very gay life.
> The day she received the news of her husband's death she accompanied three military Officers to a Hotel, a few miles outside Plymouth, and in the evening they celebrated the event by getting inebriated."

George may well have been deeply in love with Dorothy, but his feelings, it seems, were not reciprocated. In the end Dorothy was refused her pension. The record states:

> "Refuse. Say that pensions are not granted as a right, and as a result of enquiries which have been made, the Army Council are not satisfied that she is a suitable subject for this mark of royal favour."

The Foster brothers were serving with the Gordon Highlanders, and they wrote of Aubers Ridge:

> "In this attack we expended twice as much ammunition as we did at Neuve Chapelle and four times as much as in the Boer War. But the effort failed because we were short of heavy shells. The Germans were wonderfully and scientifically entrenched, and heavier shells were needed to destroy their ground works.
>
> We thought the Germans must have been annihilated, but they gave us a big surprise. The British rushed up to take the trenches, but were met with a withering fire from machine-guns which had been mounted in steel forts between the first and second line of

German trenches. There was a machine-gun about every six yards, and a murderous fire was turned on the advancing British. We failed to take the trenches and suffered many casualties.

Shortly afterwards 1,000 of our guns again bombarded the German positions, and later by a fine effort our men captured the trenches. But they were not there long, for the Germans drove them out by filling the trenches with water. The whole business was very costly for the British."

James and John Foster went on to describe in detail the ingenious arrangements which were giving the Germans supremacy:

"When the British bombarded the German trenches, the last named employed a device whereby they could let down the wire entanglements, and thus preserve them from destruction. Then, when the British infantry attacked, the wire was mechanically put into position and the poor fellows simply ran into it, in most cases with fatal consequences.

...The Germans had introduced an audacious system of spying, and in that way got hold of valuable information. One man dressed in the khaki uniform of a major was unmasked because he said he was a captain, and another regularly visited the British lines dressed as an Indian officer. Most of them speak English perfectly, and remained with the 'Tommies', in some instances for weeks. When discovered they were unceremoniously shot.

... Not long ago they were in a trench when the Germans opposite put up a notice, stating 'We are Saxons. You are Anglo-Saxons. Save your bullets for the Prussians.' The British agreed with the suggestion, and for days the troops on both sides left the trenches without being fired at. But one day the Prussians arrived, and then serious business recommenced."

Geoffrey Gwyther, serving with the Suffolk Regiment, whose cheerful boyish face smiles out of a school photograph of 1903, recounted a dramatic encounter at the end of June 1915:

"I got back into the wood at about 2.30am and found the most awful dugout reserved for me, clay walls dripping wet and only boughs overhead, which were a nest for mosquitoes. I'd only got my

Geoffrey Gwyther (right) pictured at the age of ten, shortly after his arrival at Gresham's in 1903 with his friend Eric Johnson. After the war he became an actor.

> burberry and leather and I couldn't sleep for the damp... Last night I had to take the men up again with what are called knife-rests. They are barbed wire entanglements 14ft long and 3 or 4 feet wide and high. The wire is entangled about long poles and pieces of wood. They can be carried by two men but are very heavy...It was impossible to take these knife-rests along the communication trenches as they wouldn't nearly go in, so I had to find my way across country under fire the whole time. I did it and not a man was hit, but it was pretty hot. Two men refused to come out at first, and I had to threaten to shoot the first man who spoke; I couldn't see in the dark who it was. After the first minute I was in a funny way exhilarated by it, and when I got to the end I found I was wet to the skin with perspiration."

Speech Day 1915, on 17 July, was for the most part a quiet affair at Gresham's. News of the war was having its effect. Edith, the Duchess of Hamilton, attended to present the prizes, and among her small entourage was a distinguished guest, Admiral Lord Fisher, who had recently resigned as First Sea Lord. Days after the event, the editor of *The Gresham* meditated on the good and evil associated with war and strove to find ways in which the former might outweigh the latter:

> "We can help this decision in two ways – by actually fighting and by exerting the force of public opinion in the right direction...To do this, above all we must realise the actuality of the war, and must think of it even more than we do at present – no easy task when we have no visible reminder before our eyes."

In some respects the actuality of the war seemed to be before the headmaster's eyes nonetheless. In that year of 1915 there was to be no school play, no

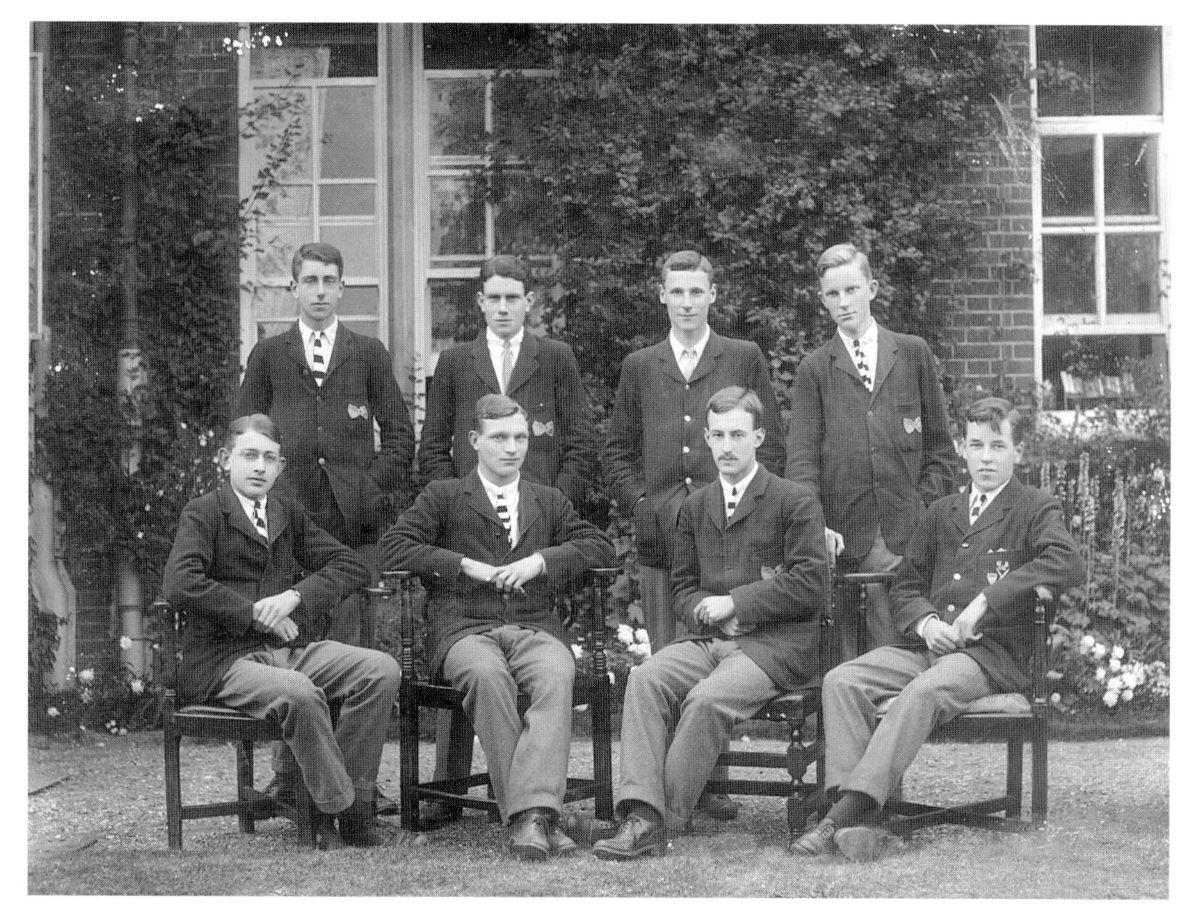

Schoolfriends and fellow house prefects in Howson's House, July 1915. Cuthbert Hill stands far right and Sebert Humphries is seated far right with David Carnegie next to him. Alleyne Boxall sits to Carnegie's right. Boxall married, in 1929, Mark and Cuthbert Hill's sister, Nina.

Shakespeare in the woods, an endeavour highly valued by Howson. It had been decided by June that no invitations were to be issued for Speech Day, that there should be no speeches and no reporters. In the event, Big School was filled by the boys, all dressed in uniform. Sir Edward Busk, the chairman of the governors, spoke briefly, reflecting on the first-class degree won by Alec Herron only a year before and "to the loss the School had sustained in his death at Neuve Chapelle".

Amongst the leaving school prefects sitting in the audience were David Carnegie and the close friends Alleyne Boxall and Cuthbert Hill. Hill was to die the following May, Carnegie in 1917, but that day they heard of the sadness of their Headmaster for those already lost.

> "Twelve of our old boys have given their lives for England. Nothing I can say will increase the honour they have won, nor lessen the sorrow of those who are left. The honour we inherit – the sorrow we fain would share. ... There must be many a fine band of Old Boys from many a school, who have given up everything to serve

> England, but to our eyes it seems impossible that there could be quite such a fine band as ours. In the haunting oppression of the war they are seldom far from the forefront of our thoughts. We do not forget."

After the prizegiving, Lord Fisher was, of course, invited to speak. The 12-year-old Geoffrey Diggle witnessed the occasion, and even at that age picked up some of the awkward nuances:

> "He launched into a blatantly egotistical speech with plenty of name-dropping: 'Once when I was having breakfast with King Edward VII…' Then he got on to Nelson. 'You boys all know his famous words, England expects every man this day will do his duty. But that is not the best thing he said. The loveliest thing he ever said was, he's a damned fool who would only fight ten ships when he had the chance of fighting against 100!' It so happened that Howson took us for his weekly Headmaster's Period next day. He asked a boy what he thought of Lord Fisher's speech, and of course received the trite answer, 'It was very good sir.' 'I cannot altogether agree with you,' observed Howson. 'Some things he said were excellent – others I wish he had left unsaid. Whether Nelson was right in calling a man a fool who preferred to fight ten ships rather than 100 is a matter of opinion, but to call him a *damned* fool was unnecessary, and did not advance his case in the slightest.'"

A long account of the Speech Day activities was given in *The Gresham*, but not one word was said about Lord Fisher, his presence or his speech.

Snipers with Green Faces

BY THE end of the summer term of 1915, many more letters had reached school, detailed and sometimes harrowing accounts of life in the trenches. Dawson Atkin wrote a long account of front-line routine from the reserve trenches while his company of The King's (Liverpool Regiment) was enjoying a rest. The mood of the writing changes rapidly, from an informative style to the abrupt reference to tragedy, and immediately afterwards to humour, as if any lengthy contemplation of the death he mentions was unbearable:

> "I usually spend most of the night fixing up iron loopholes. These must be perfectly hidden or they are very dangerous... When last in the trenches a boy in my company was shot through the head. It was on his 18th birthday. We are in reserve now having a rest. All the men are trying to learn French. You hear them asking for 'some dulay'; and 'no compri' and 'nar poo', (il n'y a plus) will be English words after the war."

He was right. The last phrase lives on in the last lines of the popular song of the time *Goodbyee*:

"So long old thing,
Cheerio, chin-chin,
Nar poo, toodle-oo
Goodbyee!"

The first time the Germans used gas, on 22 April 1915, there was, understandably, widespread panic. Kenneth Lloyd described the scene that evening:

> "About 6.30pm odd French soldiers came along with scared looks and long stories of wonderful gases. Within about half an hour it

The last school photograph of Dawson Atkin taken in July 1914 outside Woodlands.

was pretty obvious something was wrong. The French fugitives had increased to a constant stream, walking, running, riding on gun limbers and crowded in carts. Soon they were pouring over the fields as well as the roads, followed by streams of refugees trying to get their carts and stuff along in the crush. They had no officers and nothing seemed to have any power to stop them. We threatened to shoot them if they did not turn round, but they were absolutely off their heads."

Arnold Barker wrote graphically about the gas attack at Ypres on 24 May. Chlorine gas, swirling in yellow poisonous clouds, burned and destroyed the lining of the lungs. Men sometimes drowned in the fluid over-produced by their lungs to combat the chlorine, and the effects, although not always fatal, were immediate. At this time of course there were no gas masks, the best preventative a piece of water-soaked flannel over the mouth:

"Doubtless you will remember the trenches lost at Ypres on Whit Monday. We had the honour of losing them. I say honour because I think the way our boys stuck the gas was really great. I was not in the trenches at the time, but about 200 yards back in the dugouts, and I got the gas later on. It was a dreadful day. We could not get any reinforcements up and the Prussians came on, but when they got just behind the dugouts they stopped. If only they had known that we had only about half a battalion between them and Ypres, I guess the town would now be in German hands. But they did not know and, as we got the trenches back at night, it did not matter. There is, strictly speaking, no regiment of 7th D L I as we lost 700 men."

Barker's health never recovered from the effects of the gas attack. Invalided home, he later went out to Singapore in the hope that the climate would be beneficial, but he died there of a haemorrhage in 1917.

A letter reached school from Cecil Graves, from Magdeburg, dated 15 May. Along with another 38 officers he had been placed in solitary confinement, in a cell reported to be 12ft by 5ft, for 22 hours out of 24. A man of considerable inner resources, he managed to make his captivity seem almost a pleasure, such was his need to reassure those at home. At times perhaps he tried too hard:

> "You need not have the slightest anxiety about me; I am very well and cheerful and getting through a great deal of reading. My rule here is as follows: up till 1pm, that is luncheon time, I do not allow myself to open a novel, but I work at Spanish, read the German paper, and then books of history, biographies, travels etc, including Shakespeare, of which I read a little every day. I am now engaged on Carlyle and Froude, which reminds me – will you send me a short history of England? Nothing bulky, in one volume if possible... Parcels, excellent ones, came last Monday, cigarettes, a box from Fortnum and Mason, and three books...All day one looks forward to the exercise time, we walk round a court yard, each complete circle of which is 80 yards...It is a great thing for me to feel that you are not worrying about me... I am just trying to live my life as it comes, and that as well as possible."

Fortunately, Graves did not spend too long in his Magdeburg prison. By the end of July the school magazine was able to report that he was "back now at his former camp at Halle where he can be out of doors all day, and is able to get into quite good condition, as they play a good game of rounders each day and a sort of squash racquets against a wall."

After "a year of waiting and training", Mark Hill found himself in Boulogne, marching "up a most appalling hill" with a heavy pack (about 42lbs) on his back in uncomfortably hot weather. He was not enjoying himself. He wrote in his diary:

> "We arrived at 1 this morning. Reveille 5.30. Pickard and I are billeted in a room which measures 10' by 6'. He is on the floor. We might be in England for all the signs of war there are here... They say we are 20 miles from the Belgian frontier. We are all straining our ears for the sound of guns. Nearest point from here is Ypres!"

On Saturday, 31 July he wrote: "First experience of censoring letters – awful job. Also first really sound meal this side & some bridge after." He described the countryside as very pretty and the roads as good but dusty. The water supply was a problem, but "the people here are very good and obliging, & everybody is enjoying this picnic hugely." After nearly a year of warfare, and two months after the death of Julian Grenfell, who most famously used it, the 'picnic' image of war – "I adore War. It's just like a big picnic without the objectlessness of a picnic" – was still thriving.

Sunday, 1 August was "an absolutely scorching day. Church Parade in the morning & then back to billets for letters." A lengthy nosebleed followed, but:

> "The old lady here was quite too charming and gave us some wine. Somebody said they heard some guns today, which resulted in a fierce argument, expressing on the one hand a tremendous amount of local knowledge as to distances, and on the other hand a scornful incredulity applied with simply withering condescension."

An account of the argument followed:

> "'My dear fellow, it's impossible.'
> 'Oh, I don't know, at the time of Queen Victoria's funeral they heard the guns of the fleet in Leicester and that's 150 miles away, and here, according to the map we're at the very most.'
> 'Why my dear fellow,' with pipe well in the air, 'my dear fellow you'll be saying next you saw a shell pitch at Brigade HQ.'
> Someone else (a neutral) 'And a [*bloody, heavily crossed out*] good job too if it did.'"

Scribbled hurriedly at the bottom of the page are the words: "Censoring letters is an abomination." Yet Hill self-censored his diary. Was the Gresham's training still influential?

In that same July, just as he was leaving for the Front, Captain Gerald Hotblack of the Welch Regiment wrote to school to suggest that serving OGs might, as he put it, express their affection for the school by undertaking to pay for some specific part of the chapel. He felt that the war memorial proposed by the school should be a thing apart from them, made by their friends and relations, but he suggested that perhaps the seating should be theirs as a gift to the school:

> "... which has made us what we are... We do want to leave a lasting memorial of our respect and devotion which we usually find so difficult a matter to express. Most of us as soldiers have been turned out of our ordinary course of life. We have lost many of our old financial responsibilities. In such a time we would do our work without pay. We ought not to lose this opportunity – it will never come again – of expressing our affection for the school... In times such as these all OGs cannot help thinking of the School which some of us will never see again."

Two such died in the Dardanelles within two days of each other in August, in the second British landing, the great attack on Suvla Bay, which claimed thousands of lives. Lieutenant Ian Maclean Wilson's battalion of the Yorkshire Regiment landed at Suvla Bay at about 9pm on 6 August and was ordered to take the small hill of Lala Baba. They had not gone far when "they came upon a trench full of Turks and it was here that he fell at the head of his men."
A fellow officer wrote:

> "The men were simply splendid. You would be sorry to hear about Wilson. He died bravely leading his men up to the attack of Lala Baba. He fell just in front of the top trench on the hill, and from what I can make out must have died practically instantaneously. He was a nice fellow and his platoon was very cut up at losing him. I heard one of his men say that he was a little hero and led his men splendidly."

His father wrote to the War Office:

> "I hope later to hear from you or from some of his brother officers some details of how he died and how he did his duty. He was our only boy, but neither his mother nor myself have any regrets that he gave himself to his king and country. He had a happy though short life and a glorious end, and we must bear our loss as patiently as we can."

When his son's effects were not forthcoming after several weeks his father wrote again, commenting: "I know there may be a difficulty as nearly all the officers have been wiped out." Such were the circumstances of war in Gallipoli.

Two days after Wilson's death, Edward Andrews, a private in the New Zealand

Expeditionary Force, lost his life in Gallipoli, in an attack on the heights of Chunuk Bair. A week later, G. R. Day, a master at Gresham's until 1912, and also in the Suvla Bay landings, was wounded by rifle bullets in four places within 20 minutes.

Alan Jarvis was also in the Dardanelles, serving as a captain with the Middlesex Regiment, and decided to write to the school magazine about the campaign there "as everyone seems to be in Flanders."

> "Out here the fighting is very different. We have just effected a new landing, and on the Peninsula we have no luxurious dugouts, no A.S.C. [*Army Service Corps*] to bring us a variety of food, no letters, mails or papers. Nothing seems to reach us and we, at present, have to live on bully beef and very hard biscuits. To drink we delight in very muddy water that leaves a sediment in your mouth, leaving you even more thirsty. It is appallingly hot by day, and bitterly cold during the night. In spite of these odds we have advanced several miles, and are very well established. In a few days I expect things will be working very well. I have just heard that Snelling [*another OG*] is close by with the R.A.M.C. We have suffered rather badly, and have lost several officers and a great number of men. Snipers painted green effect big losses among the officers. A few days ago a woman sniper was actually found and she had 14 identity discs round her neck; presumably she had crawled out at night and taken them off her victims! I am now using my machine-guns to clear the trees of them. I had great difficulty in getting the guns up at all, as we have no transport, and everything at present is carried by hand."

Another Greshamian, Thomas Baines, echoed much of Jarvis's description of life in the peninsula – the snipers with green faces, the dreadful food and lack of hot tea, the inadequate transport. After only one morning of fighting he was shot in both legs by machine-gun fire, more fortunate, though, than many. "At the end of the day we had five officers left out of 23."

By the middle of 1915, still serving on the Western Front, Second-Lieutenant Dawson Atkin of The King's (Liverpool Regiment), whose capacity for being cheerful seems to have been remarkable, was discovering:

> "This is a very interesting life. It is very interesting to study the different types of men we have in the regiment and, if tired of them

> we are always near the Highland Light Infantry, who all go by the name of 'Jock'. There are also the 1/1st Gurkhas and the 27th Punjabis. On our left now are the 40th Pathans, commonly called the '40 Thieves.' These nations differ greatly and all have their food laws. They are a very jolly lot altogether."

The autumn campaign around Ypres was very much a continuation of that of the spring, but now penetrating southward into Champagne. Because of a delay to accommodate the long pre-attack bombardment demanded by Petain, the Germans were well able to prepare their defence. There were two lines, with a row of concrete machine-gun posts in between, with the artillery instructed to fire on the advancing infantry. Any who survived that met a hail of machine-gun fire. The so-called "battle" of Loos began on 25 September. It has been claimed that this chaotic and disastrous action was dignified and flattered by the suggestion that it was an organised, focused "battle" rather than a string of ill- co-ordinated events.

Matters went wrong from the start when a discharge of retaliatory chlorine gas, used for the first time by the British, drifted back into the British trenches. Stanley Armitage, a corporal in the 9th Division of the KRRC, was one of thousands killed on that first day. Also involved in the battle was William Barker, the elder brother of Arnold Barker, who, like Arnold, was serving with the DLI, but had been in France only a few weeks. A major in the 15th Division DLI wrote to William Barker's father in November 1915, describing the events at Loos. Even he did not call it a battle:

> "I have been anxious to write and tell you how very gallantly and nobly your son behaved in the terrible engagement of Loos. Terrible as a test for green troops, but very nearly magnificent as a feat of arms I suppose.
>
> I have not been able to put my feelings into words. If I tell you he was perfectly cool and self-possessed in the most trying of circumstances, and utterly unselfish and unmindful of his own safety in his regard for that of others, it would but ill convey my meaning. It would not tell you of his tender solicitude for me.
>
> When I was weak and faint from loss of blood I did my utmost to persuade him to leave me but he would not. He propped me up and half dragged me across an open stretch of country under fire and into a trench, and later on he again helped me along through the streets of Loos during a terrible bombardment."

The writer went on to describe "a magnificent piece of cool calculating bravery". The trench they occupied had been dug by the enemy, and thus the entrance was facing the wrong way. Shots came in that way and were also flying all around. Both men had been hurt. The balance of probability seemed to be that the Germans were holding the nearby trenches and that they were in imminent danger of capture if they stayed much longer where they were. In this crisis, a decision had to be made quickly. Barker took it, and luck was with him:

> "He went, armed with my revolver, under fire for 100 to 120 yards and there he found a Scottish Company. Then he came all the way back to the dugout, and, as I said, remained to the very last to help me along."

After the first two devastating days, at the end of which the German machine-gunners – out of mercy – held their fire as the British retreated, the fighting in the area continued for another three weeks. At the end of that time the British had lost 16,000 soldiers, with a further 25,000 wounded.

Mark Hill had arrived in France with his regiment, the 6th Leicesters, only weeks before Loos. Among Mark's papers is a collection of poems, some favourites of his – Kipling's *If* for example – and some composed by him. One, entitled *25th September 1915*, clearly refers to Loos, and embodies a bitterness and crude hatred unique in Mark Hill's collection of writings:

> "1.
> We like to honour the foe we fight –
> But –
> If you had been where we have been,
> If you had seen what we have seen,
> If you had felt what we had felt,
> If you had smelt what we have smelt, -
> Would you be careful + gentle + kind
> And consider the Swine and his frame of mind?
> If your heart was right
> You'd bayonet the brute with all your might.
> 2.
> What a terrible game it is, by fate!
> Hunting and killing the foe you hate;
> Crashing a bayonet clean through a Hun,

> Or racing a belt through a Maxim gun,
> Giving him back what he gave to you
> In the early days when the shells were few.
> If you had been caught in gas and fire
> Would you get up + say 'I admire'?
> Not on your life,
> If your heart was right
> You'd bayonet the brute with all your might."

As the autumn wore on, Lieutenant Jasper Phillimore, formerly of Gresham's, St Augustine's College, Canterbury and a Bachelor of Science of University College London, fell in a charge made by the Buffs near Vermelles on 13 October. Vermelles was destroyed in the fighting of 1915, described two years later by Claude Rouse as a "poor place, no whole houses exist, and great shell holes in the streets tell the tale of how fierce and sanguinary must have been the battles." The lieutenant-colonel commanding the 6th Buffs wrote a letter to Phillimore's father, revealing, unusually, the difficulties of his current circumstances:

> "Under considerable stress, I am writing to tell you that our Phillimore was as gallant as any British Officer could be and his loss to the Battalion will be hard to replace. I thank God he has been buried within our lines and that it will be possible to identify his grave."

By October 1915, Gerald Hotblack's suggestion of July had been taken up enthusiastically. A group of 37 OG school prefects had by that time signed a letter inviting their fellows to contribute to a fund to provide the stalls seating and panelling of the new chapel.

> "In these days we are proud of the school, and of the fact that 70% of her Old Boys are serving the King. And it seems to us that there could be no more fitting tribute than that we should complete the Chapel at this moment, when so many OGs have already gone, or are preparing to go, to the Front. For the Chapel will be the heart and centre of the School, and to complete it would bind us together in a lasting way."

Of the 34 subscribers whose names were listed below the letter, 13 were to die in the war, and in that sense they were contributing to their own memorial. Their

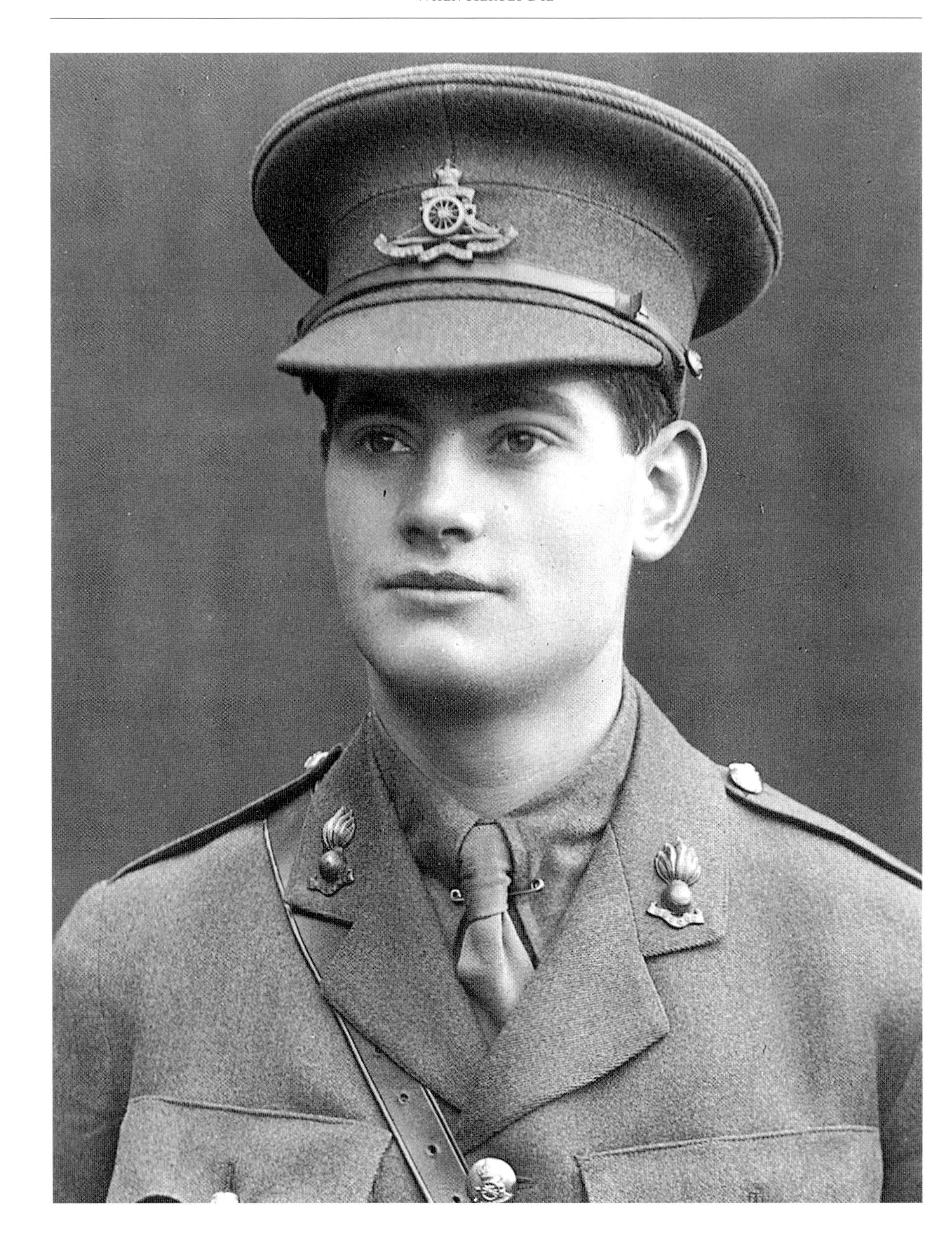

names, with many more of the fallen, are carved on the fine oak stalls, "binding them together" according to their wish, for as long as the chapel stands.

One of the signatories of the letter, Frank Halsey, was killed on 14 November, the victim of a shell which exploded in his dugout. Halsey was serving as a second-lieutenant with the 3rd Trench Mortar Battery, Royal Garrison Artillery. Trench mortar teams were nicknamed the "Suicide Club" as they were favoured German targets once they had revealed their whereabouts. Halsey had been at Loos and wrote a letter back to school about it, minimising the losses and giving great credit to others for bravery. The most interesting section concerns the use of mortars. Mortars were known as "the pocket artillery". Only 545 were fired by the British in 1914, but Halsey's letter was prophetic in that in 1916 their worth had been realised and six and a half million were fired in that year:

Frank Halsey, who died in November 1915. He was deeply mourned by Howson, who had chosen him as his head of school in 1912.

> "My mortars are splendid little affairs; unfortunately there exists a deplorable ignorance as to their capabilities amongst superior officers of all kinds, and I do not think we are given the opportunities which we could undoubtedly improve. A weapon which can throw 4lbs of high explosive 700 yards, and can be carried, ammunition and all, by five men for nearly half a mile at a quick walk, is a factor deserving of more recognition than it gets...
> I spoke to some prisoners; they said they had been at the Front only three days, had been forced to go forward by an officer with a revolver, and had all left wives behind in Schleswig. They were middle-aged Landsturm men, and seemed very shaken."

Halsey had been working in Munich when war broke out, so he presumably had a good command of German. His stay in Munich came as a direct result of his unusual academic ability. Even before he was 18, Frank Halsey had gained a Demyship (scholarship) in Natural Science at Magdalen College Oxford. This must have been particularly pleasing to Howson, as he wished in later life that he himself had held the same scholarship in the same college. It was considered that in view of Halsey's youth he would benefit from continuing at school for another year. There he assisted his chemistry master, himself a former Demy, and presumably another strong influence, in chemical research. Frank Halsey did so well in chemistry and mathematics that when he went up to Oxford the following year, he could begin by undertaking third-year work. Because he was so far ahead, he spent the summer of 1914 at Munich University.

It is hard to avoid the conclusion that he had much to give the world had he not lost his life in war. The Magdalen College Register records the gift of the photograph sent by his mother, a widow, in 1919 and the words of his "Mention in Despatches", conventional enough in themselves no doubt, but representing much courage and dedication:

> "At all times and under all circumstances he showed a brave and indomitable spirit combined with an energy and devotion to duty which could not be excelled."

His effects reveal an interest in religion less conventional, including as they did not only a bible and a "small devotional book", but also three Christian Science books.

A tribute in *The Gresham* was almost certainly contributed by Howson, whose head of school Halsey had been in 1912:

> "One cannot picture Frank Halsey as dead. Life, colour, running water, the wind on the heath, sunlit gorse, the song of birds, will always speak of him to those who knew him best... Many remember with pleasure his first solo at a school concert, and the simplicity with which he played, a tiny boy perched out of reach of the pedals... As Captain of his House, as Captain of the School, he inspired a sense of trust that could not question – his loyalty was wonderful."

An Oxford friend wrote touchingly:

> He has gone on.
> For him no splendid comradeship in death
> With heroes of high contests like the Marne;
> Not his an end beneath a dawning sky
> In some fierce fight more ultimate and easterly:
> The world marks but another soldier dead,
> The daily toll that keeps our Line inviolate.
> But we who knew him here, who shared with him
> The watches of another service, we see more.
> His name upon our walls, imperishable,
> Fragments he wrote, the work he did so well,
> The shadow of his presence still with us,
> Tell us of what he was and what he would have been.

Only a week later, Captain Geoffrey Barham Johnson lost his life. As a young boy, Geoffrey Johnson had been a chorister at Windsor and had attended, among other state occasions, the Coronation of Edward VII in 1902. He had also subsequently enjoyed a very successful time at Gresham's, where he was captain of his house and captain of football (rugby). He went from school to Jesus College, Cambridge, where, between his rowing and his rugby, he read for Holy Orders. At the outbreak of war he was gazetted to the 7th Battalion of the Norfolk Regiment, as he was a native of East Dereham. Before he went to the Front he was promoted captain, and in September 1915 he became company commander. The 7th Battalion of the Norfolks was something of a "Gresham's" battalion in that two other old boys also served in it, Charles Shepherd and Humphrey Thorn. One of them wrote to school that Johnson "died as he lived, doing his duty; a gallant officer and a man."

Geoffrey Barham Johnson, killed in 1915, a captain in the 7th Battalion, Norfolk Regiment. The regiment also included two more of the Gresham's fallen, Humphrey Thorn and Charles Shepherd.

Johnson was killed by a rifle grenade whilst handing over to the Royal Berkshire Regiment at Vermelles on 22 November 1915. They apparently arrived an hour early and a degree of confusion ensued in which "Johnnie" Johnson, as he was known, was killed. A fellow lieutenant wrote to Johnson's parents:

> "He was simply loved by all from the lowest to the highest, but no one will miss him more than myself. I happened to be in the trenches when he was wounded and at once went down to see if there was anything I could do. I found him badly hit but conscious. In spite of everything being done that was possible, he died soon afterwards. He was perfectly calm and brave the whole time... We buried him the following day at 3 o'clock at Vermelles, in the British cemetery."

He lies there still, with Jasper Phillimore and Frank Halsey nearby.

The last days of the year brought two more Greshamian deaths. On 30 December 1915, Joseph Simpson was killed in the explosion of the HMS *Natal*. The *Natal* was a cruiser, at the time in the Cromarty Firth. A fire began on board, quickly igniting the ammunition stored below decks, shooting flames up the main mast and causing a massive explosion. Not all the men on board were lost, but there were 304 deaths, with those surviving being very badly burned.

Norman Ayris fell on the last day of 1915. Before the war he trained as an engineer and in 1914 he received his commission in the Royal Engineers. The tributes to him reveal an optimistic character "so full of life and energy, and so keen on his work". At the time of his death he was engaged in "dangerous but necessary work" and one evening about 10pm he was caught in a sudden burst of rifle fire and died "almost instantaneously". The word "almost" has a sinister ring. The key to his indomitable personality may have lain in circumstances tantalisingly suggested, but not explained, by a fellow OG:

> "Confronted with apparently insurmountable difficulties from his childhood, he was not disheartened, but, always looking on the bright side of things, he ultimately overcame them all and passed on triumphant. He was without a trace of selfishness, and by his cheery manner did much to encourage others."

In terms of the Gresham's record, it was a grim way to end the year.

Thy Will Be Done

ON THE morning of Sunday, 23 January 1916, Archdeacon Westcott of Norwich consecrated the new chapel at Gresham's School. With winter sunlight flooding the building, "gilding the grand oak roof in a remarkable manner", the Archdeacon preached the sermon. He commented:

> "This chapel is linked in time and memory with the devastating struggle for life and liberty and righteousness and honour and all that men hold dearest… Not a few who did their part towards the willing sacrifice embodied in these walls, have laid at the feet of God, and at the feet of the Mother Country a far more costly offering. God knows you would like to have these schoolfellows still

The interior of the school chapel pictured as it was at the time of its consecration in January 1916. Already by that time plans were well under way to create a memorial to the boys who had fallen in the war.

> of your body on earth, with all their youthful vigour, and generous enthusiasm. But so was not 'The Will.'"

Evensong that same afternoon was at three o'clock. This time the headmaster preached, taking as his text Matthew vi.10, "Fiat Voluntas Tua – Thy will be done." It was fitting in several ways that this sentence should be the inspiration for the sermon. As the motto of Sir John Gresham, the founder of the school, it was placed in iron on the south door and written in stained glass on the window of the ante-chapel. As an expression of achievement in the building of the chapel in such difficult circumstances it gave the honour to God. As a guide to living through the Great War, it reflected an attitude of passive suffering in the face of the enormity of mass slaughter, but also, suggested the headmaster, a way of participating "in God's purposes… as a doer of His will." Howson's struggle to find positive messages for his boys amid the disasters and losses of war was clear:

> "Some of you, if need be, will go with courage and readiness to face death. But for most, perhaps for all, a more splendid opportunity for love and devotion is waiting, to face life…"

Howson was always anxious to hear news of his boys, and throughout the war he tried to maintain contact with as many of them as he could. His sister Rosa seems to have done much of the "secretarial" work in fact, although Howson himself was an enthusiastic host to the many OGs who visited and stayed with him in Holt while they were on leave. In a letter in *The Gresham* of February 1916 he wrote:

> "The days on which I receive letters from 'Old Boys' are better than other days. The doings of OGs are of deep interest to many here. I should be glad to hear from 'Old Boys' of their doings and experiences."

Howson's biographer commented in 1925 that Howson's determination to follow the wartime careers of the boys wore him out. Although his sister undoubtedly helped with his correspondence, when a former pupil of Gresham's was killed it was of course Howson himself who wrote to the parents, and there is no doubt of his sincerity. A schoolmaster in Howson's mode, whose emotional life was centred on his boys, who lived with them in a boarding house during term and took them with him on fishing holidays to Wharfedale, "the nearest thing to home life that he knew", was likely to be deeply affected by the loss of so many whom he had known so well. At school, a weekly intercession service was held in the chapel on Thursday evenings, at which the lengthening list of boys who had lost their lives was read out. For the headmaster these must have been gruelling occasions.

By April 1916 the editor of the school magazine could write:

> "The past few weeks have seen the most prolonged and fierce battle of the greatest war in history. It has been said, we hope with truth, that it is the last effort of the enemy..."

It was not to be. The Verdun Offensive, although a German failure, was not the enemy's last gasp, and the summer saw the beginning of the Somme Offensive, planned in part to divert attention from Verdun, although in historical terms infamous for its miscalculations and consequent shattering losses.

Before that, in May, David Dulley, a corporal with the Lincolnshire Regiment, died in France of pneumonia, a reminder of the huge losses in the war which were caused by disease rather than bullets and shells.

News also arrived at school about that time of Hans Busk, who had been reported missing some months previously, in early January. Busk had been a student at King's College, Cambridge, from October 1912 until the spring of

The wrecked plane of Hans Busk, January 1915. He lived to play an important role in Gallipoli, but met his death a year later.

Hans Busk (centre) in Imbros, Gallipoli, with 2 Wing RNAS 1915.

1914. He left college six months before the war began to join the Royal Naval Air Service and became a pilot and flight commander. From the outset he had some frightening moments. The *Dundee Courier* reported a narrow escape in January 1915.

Hans and a fellow officer had gone out on an observation flight at eight in the morning when the engine of his seaplane failed in a strong wind. Once on the surface "the wind shrieked through the plane supports and wave after wave dashed against the machine which was swung about like a cork". Eventually, with the seaplane by now upside down and the airmen clinging to the floats, they were able to signal to the shore, a signal picked up by a member of the Highland Cyclists' Brigade patrolling the shore near the village of Kingsbarns. He summoned the help of three fishermen in the yawl *Barbara*, who "with a mere rag for a sail" rescued the freezing men and took them safely back to St Andrews.

In the summer of 1915, Busk was sent to the Mediterranean, being engaged mainly in flights over Gallipoli and raids over the Turkish mainland. After his disappearance in early January 1916, his kit, containing a pocket book with some diary jottings, had been returned from the island of Imbros, in the Dardanelles. Hans Busk played a very important role in attempting to provide air cover for the evacuation of thousands of Allied soldiers from Suvla Bay, and the comments in his notebook refer to the last weeks before he went missing, particularly of his exploits in December 1915. His observations, recorded in a laconic style, registered his relish at the fate of the Turks:

> "Destroyer came along level to shore full bat at 440 yards, then loosed off at Turk's trenches at about 30 shots per minute!… Whole thing took about 5 minutes – very pretty sight from air."

Now and then he logged his total of flying hours – 26, 29, 37, 39, 41, 47. On 23 December he recorded:

> "Anzac is a proper rabbit warren of dugouts. Hills extremely high and steep… Forgot to mention have taken charge of flying new pilots. They are not much use."

This may have been the arrogance of a veteran, but there may also have been a strong element of objective truth in the remark.

His entry for 29 December describes an exciting and frightening dogfight with a jammed gun and anti-aircraft fire making life very difficult for Busk:

> "He got us in several places with a long shot – one came through the nacelle, made a hole in Edwards' trousers, then entered my coat above the elbow of the right arm and came out again at the wrist, badly bruising my arm. It made a fearful din and felt like an enormous thing!"

This account seems to bear out fully the assessment of him which appeared in the King's College annual report: "His cool, light-hearted daring and resource were conspicuous." One week later Busk's luck ran out. On 6 January he did not return from a flight. He was carrying a 550lbs bomb destined for an enemy aerodrome and so was in an aircraft, a Henry Farman biplane described as reliable but not fast (about 70mph), alone because of the weight. This in turn meant that he did not have a gun, as he could not have fired it whilst flying the plane. A search revealed nothing, but it was thought that he may have been forced down by anti-aircraft fire and been taken prisoner. For many months the hope that he had survived was kept alive, but finally, in July 1919, three years later, it was acknowledged that he must have been brought down over the sea, although his exact fate was never established.

His commander wrote affectionately of him:

> "He worked most tremendously hard and was always flying as we were so short-handed. He formed one of my small band of pilots who were second to none, and I don't suppose anyone nowadays [*1919*] realises what the nation owes to him and three or four others. When I look back and remember the aeroplanes they had to fly over miles of sea, and face very heavy and accurate anti-aircraft fire continuously and at low altitudes, it seems extraordinary that we lasted so long."

The pressure on these pilots flying day after day in such dangerous conditions was immense. The month of January 1916 was notable for its losses of aircrew in Gallipoli. Busk was the first of seven to die in those few weeks.

In France, Atkin was keeping up his spirits despite adverse circumstances. As ever, his letter combines humour and horror in close proximity. The dangerous night raid, and reference to identifying a German regiment, is strongly reminiscent of a scene in the play by Richard Sherriff, *Journey's End.*

> "I am billeted at present just within range of the small German Howitzers. It is a small village on the main pavé road, so about 50 per cent of the houses are estaminets. They give us about 20 shells a week. Little damage is done except to inhabitants. The windows of rooms occupied by inhabitants are usually broken, chiefly by the concussion, because they always keep them tightly shut. A French newspaper boy has just passed. He has a donkey cart pulled by three dogs. As well as being very intelligent, by keeping out of the way of carts etc. they can take him along at about 8 miles an hour.
>
> You would laugh to see me and my horse Joe together (everyone does). I think it has a paternal feeling towards me, for it has never yet thrown me (as it does most). But even so it takes a few minutes' argument to get it past crossroads. It has a wonderful memory and loves to take you to your billet of months before.
>
> If it ever gets into the papers, you may read of 'a successful raid on enemy trenches'. Everyone, except those who have to do them, is very keen on them. We did one, at least all I did was to keep a gun firing over their heads to make enough noise to cover the sound of the wire cutters. I think those that did it deserve the highest praise. Most of these raids develop into throwing a few bombs into the enemy's wire, and then getting home as fast as possible. Our raid (of course) was very different. For five nights their wire was examined

> by patrols. On the night a telephone was taken out and three men cut the wire, shoulder to shoulder for three and a half hours. This was done on marshy ground, with a very cold wind and frequent showers of sleet. The men were so cold that they had to be dragged in. Then six men went forward and lay at the foot of the parapet for an hour, waiting for the German officer on duty to come round. The trench there was almost full of water, and the officer walking on the parapet came within three feet of the party. The men were so cold that they were almost helpless; however one of them managed to kill the officer with his bayonet, and he fell into the trench. The object of the raid was to bring home a live Hun, or at least get something by which the Hun regiment could be identified. In this they failed, since rapid fire was opened on them from the sentry posts on both sides. Three of the six were wounded and the other three had all they could do to bring them in. One of these three died of wounds and exposure afterwards. All came in looking like lumps of mud. The Huns ever since have been very nervy and have been sending up lights the whole time (I don't blame them).
>
> We all look very weird now that we have to wear these tin shrapnel helmets. They are a very good idea, since we have had many men killed by shrapnel bullets and pieces of H.E. [*Heavy Explosive*] falling, that have been going just hard enough to penetrate the skull. They also give greater confidence."

They may have given greater confidence, but for many they did not prevent fatal wounds to the head. It is however extraordinary to think that for so long soldiers were facing so much ordnance with so little protection.

Harlowe Lowe was building miles of wire entanglements along the third line of defence in his sector:

> "Part of the line ran through a British and Indian cemetery, where there were many graves. It was rather a sad place, but the graves are kept splendidly with a cross bearing an inscription over each and many have wreaths and flowers placed on them by the French peasants. I had a look round but did not see the graves of any OGs there."

Shortly afterwards Lowe was moved about six miles nearer the line to make dugouts and to repair the trenches which were "very bad in this part of the line".

Because it was too dangerous to work during the day, all this was done at night:

> "We usually leave here about 7pm and get back between 2 and 2.30 in the morning. We are billeted about five miles from the trenches and for the first ten days we had to walk all the way there and back every night besides doing all the work when we got there. But now I am glad to say we have six motor buses which take us just over half way there, and fetch us at 2am so this is a great boon…"

Meanwhile Edward Giles was notching up his flying hours (at the time of his writing, 24) and described a hazardous 20 minutes facing six German aircraft while on a patrol. He was explaining for those at home the features of the plane he flew:

> "If a machine attacks from the back, the observer can turn round and fire the gun over the pilot's head, as this gun is on a swivelling mounting. If one attacks from the side he can take his gun and put it on a mounting at the side. This may sound very easy, but it is not when one is bundled up in leather clothes in a very cramped place, with an 80 mile wind in one's face, especially to a person like myself, who was never very graceful or smart in my movements. However, a hostile machine in the vicinity works wonders, and one can throw oneself about in quite an astonishing way."

At the end of May came the Battle of Jutland. Cuthbert Hill was lost with his ship, HMS *Invincible*, on 31 May 1916. The *Invincible*, a battle cruiser, was blown up when enemy damage set alight charges in the handling rooms. The same design fault which allowed the explosion in a damaged gun turret to ignite the shells in the magazine below the gun had already in that same battle led to the loss of the *Queen Mary* and the *Indefatigable*. Broken in two, the *Invincible*, grotesquely belying its name, sank in 15 seconds. Of the 1,031 men on board, only six survived.

At school Cuthbert Hill had been an important figure – a house and school prefect, keen on games and acting. Perhaps as important, he had been in the words of a contemporary struggling with homesickness, "a nice boy". The memoirs of the homesick child (written in the 1970s) give a glimpse of the conventions of public school life at the time. On his first day at Gresham's Junior School, Alan Dane, at that time aged 12, recalled:

> "Finally a boy about nine months younger than myself, who lived at Northwood where I lived and whom I knew slightly, came up to me. 'Hello Cuthy,' I said. Cuthy drew back. 'Sh,' he said, 'you must call me Hill Minor now.' So that was that."

But it was not quite. Even though Dane apparently found his companions "uninteresting", he went for walks on Sunday afternoons with Cuthy and another boy, played cricket with them and accompanied them to chapel. He was also invited to study tea with Cuthbert's elder brother Marco.

From school, Cuthbert had passed by special entry into the Royal Navy and gone to Keyham. His death provoked an outpouring of grief recorded in *The Gresham*, which despite having no attribution was probably the work of Howson himself:

> "Memory will long mark the charm of May 1916 with a white stone, and few at Holt will easily forget the week in which Cuthbert Hill was amongst us 'on leave'. Even those who had not known him before were glad to see him. He was good to look on and his face faithfully reflected his character. Few records can be as fair as his. As a House Prefect and as a School Prefect his judgment was valued because it implied clearness and justice. His word was the word of an Englishman. His selflessness, his silent influence, were remarkable. He knew what was right and did it."

Cuthbert himself wrote to his mother about that leave spent in Holt, in letters dated 14 and 16 May 1916. He speaks in the first about going to Newcastle to see Boxall. The reference is to Alleyne Boxall, a great school friend of his. The families became linked even more closely in 1929, when Alleyne married Nina Hill, the sister of Cuthbert and Mark. The letter went on:

> "It was not very nice here yesterday but was fine enough for cricket. I bowled 5 wides in one over, why I was put on I don't know, but I made up for it by making 61 which pleased me very much indeed. There was early service in the Chapel and of course I had to read the lesson. As a matter of fact I don't mind it so much now..."

Two days later, the story was much the same. More cricket – "did not do much" – dinner at Crossways – "they only have two candles on the table as the police object if they have their light on" – and a ride on a motor bike belonging to one of the masters – "it was great fun and I went all round the place. I am having a great time" – completed his visit.

By 23 May he had joined his ship, writing to his mother more details of his time in Holt:

> "The Head went up to town on Thursday and he asked me to take his work and also prep. I believe that he would have liked me to take prayers, but that was too much. The work was geography about longitude and time. I am afraid that I would not make a very good schoolmaster."

On 28 May he wrote his last letter to his "Dear Mummie", on paper headed "HMS Invincible." In it he speaks of "regular Scotch mists" at sea, and of his friend Boxall, whose active war service was to begin almost exactly as Cuthbert's ended:

> "He has lent me his Mo-Bike while he is away and it is at present waiting for me till we go back… I will write again some time in the middle of the week. Love to all. Heaps and heaps of Love from your loving son Cuthbert."

He was, after all, only 18.

After the news of the Battle of Jutland broke, his elder brother Laurie wrote desperately (and he felt inarticulately), to their mother:

> "We mustn't give up hope while there is the faintest chance left, and at present there must be a very good chance… How I wish I were with you now. I'm afraid I never have been able to say what I feel but I know you will understand.
> If the worst has happened and Cuthie has given his life for his country, it is a thing to be proud of for all time. That the youngest should have been chosen for this honour, before even he was tried, seems horribly hard, yet it does not alter the glorious fact – he gave all for England. There can be no better thing than this.
> How proud dear old Dad would have been."

A few days later, in a letter written in pencil on rough squared paper, probably torn from his field service note book, headed only "Trenches" and dated cursorily "7.6.16", Mark Hill tried to put words to his terrible grief in his letter to his mother:

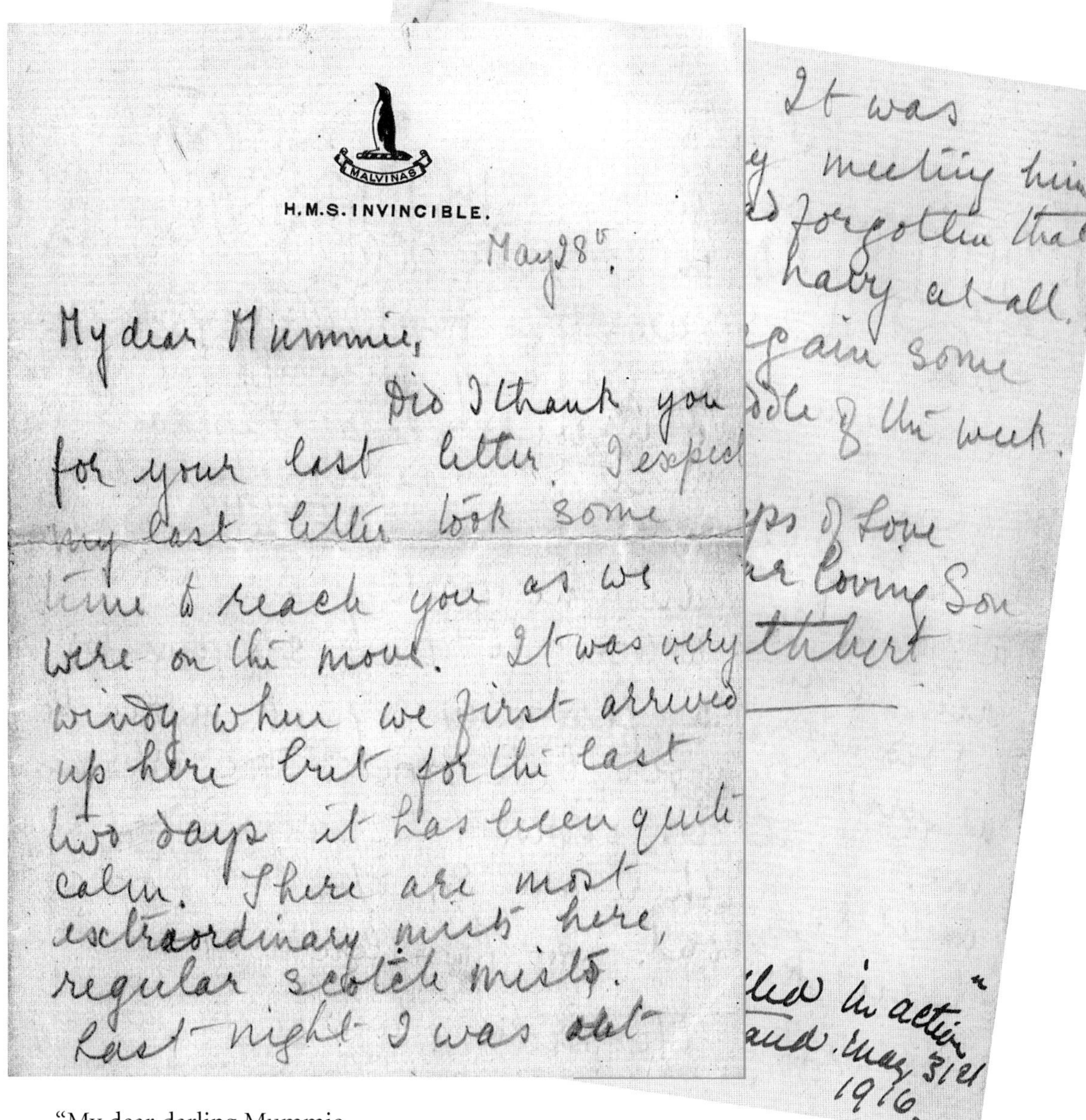

MALVINAS

H.M.S. INVINCIBLE.

May 28th.

My dear Mummie,

Did I thank you for your last letter. I expect my last letter took some time to reach you as we were on the move. It was very windy when we first arrived up here but for the last two days it has been quite calm. There are most extraordinary mists here, regular scotch mists.

Last night I was abt

It was
y meeting him
d forgotten that
navy at all.
gain some
ddle of the week.
ps of Love
r Loving Son
thbert

led in action"
and. May 31st
1916.

Cuthbert Hill's last letter to his mother written on headed notepaper from HMS *Invincible.* Three days later he was killed in the Battle of Jutland.

"My dear darling Mummie,

I have just got your letter. I saw about the battle 2 days ago but cheated myself into the belief that Cuthbert was still on leave. But now the lists are out so I was expecting and very much afraid of your letter today.

It is no use, dear darling Mummie, my trying to put anything down on paper because you know I can't put what I really think. At present I can hardly think it even. It seems incredible that so much embodied love & affection, such bright and limitless possibilities, such expressions of face & speech, such marked individuality should at one blow cease to be a factor in our lives & become an intangible memory. Dear Mummie, I know how lovable he was to me and so I can realise how impossible it would be for me even to guess at what this means for you.

You know how much I hate all sentimentality. I find it difficult to speak of a tearing wrenching grief like this. Of all of us, except yourself, I have probably been closer to him all our lives at school and home & I know exactly his high place. I have always thought – if I can do as well as Laurie I shall be satisfied – and lately, as I watched Cuthie I thought – if I can take as high a place as he will in life I shall be happy. Well, I have as high an aim – to live and die as worthy of you as he did – as ever I thought possible.

I hope you will read behind these stupid words & see, as I mean you to, no washy sentiment but a realisation of this simple tragedy the glory of which has really thrilled me.

Beauty, uprightness, enthusiasm, love – love to give and love to inspire – these do not die, but live on in all our hearts which come into contact with them.

Think of the wide circle of his friends at Holt to which the sight and thought of him would send a generous glow to the heart & give rise to such love and friendship – & you will realise that here was a life through whom it pleased God to be very, very generous to the world. Well, he has reclaimed the gift. "All which I took from thee, I did but take, not for thy harms, But just that thou might seek them in my arms."

Mummie, I am feeling very, very unhappy for you, but you should be feeling so much prouder than even I am feeling.

I could do great things today through the inspiration of great thoughts, one of the greatest of which is that I love you.

Marco."

At school, Cuthbert's friends too were feeling his loss. One, Sebert Humphries, wrote in June to Mrs Hill thanking her for her letter and the promise of a photograph:

"The Head preached tonight and spoke of Cuthie: it was rather moving, as he meant what he said, and we knew that what he said was true… I do hope Cuthie can know what a help he is being, and always will be, to at least one of his friends: he must know."

The headmaster's words about Cuthbert impressed another pupil, the young Geoffrey Diggle.

> "A short time ago you had the privilege of being taken by Hill. I have just heard that he has died for his country. I never heard him tell a lie or commit a mean action."

Mark Hill's letter to his mother from the trenches, June 1916, expressing his grief at his brother's death.

Trenches
7/6/16.
My dear darling Mummie,
I have just got your letter. I saw about the battle 2 days ago but cheated myself into the belief that Cuthbert was still on leave. But now the lists are out so I was expecting & very much afraid of your letter to-day.
It is no use, dear darling Mummie, my trying to put anything down on paper, because you know I can't put what I really think at present. I can hardly think even. It seems incredible that so much embodied love & affection such bright & limitless possibilities such expressions of fact & speech, such marked individuality, should, at one blow cease to be a factor in our lives & become an intangible memory. Dear Mummie I know how lovable he was to me & so I can realize how

On 14 July, Bastille Day, a day of celebration for the French even in the midst of war, Mark Hill was killed near Bazentin, surviving his brother by only about six weeks. He was serving as a lieutenant with the 6th Battalion Leicester Regiment, and the action in which he died happened on the same day as the disastrous attack on High Wood in which Mark's schoolfellow, Dawson Atkin, suffered the wounds which caused his death two days later. Mark was another of the Gresham's elite. A captain of School House and a school prefect, his presence on so many photographs attests to his sporting prowess, talents matched by intellectual ability. He had gone up to Magdalene College Cambridge on an Exhibition to read for the Natural Science Tripos in October 1913, but joined up and gained his commission immediately war broke out in August 1914. In October 1915 he had suffered at a sniper's hand a severe perforating bullet wound to his right knee which went straight through the joint leaving it permanently stiff, but he was killed before his request for a wound pension could be dealt with. His last letter to his mother spoke of letters received from Mr Howson and Mr Eccles, and of a humorous incident during church parade:

> "Just when the padre got to the point where, with one hand in the air, he was saying 'and fire and brimstone came down from heaven', a large piece of shell fell just a few yards behind him. It was so extraordinarily well-timed that it quite put him out of step."

His last words were of the future:

> "There is tremendous optimism here; things really are going to happen this year."

The affection in which both Mark and Cuthbert were held at school is striking. A tribute to Mark to which several of his friends contributed reveals the engaging character of the man. "An absolutely exceptional fellow." "His cheery personality was always a joy". "Entirely sincere and right-minded." Perhaps the most touching and certainly the most personal comment may have been the contribution from his headmaster: "Slow to seize a point of humour, he thoroughly enjoyed the effort and gave and felt much joy when he rippled to the surface, grasping it." Alan Dane, whose praise for anyone at Gresham's was usually muted, compared Mark with himself, to his own disadvantage:

> "Marco was a fine healthy boy, gifted in powers, an excellent actor, intelligent and with what I lacked, a strong sense of public-spiritedness. He was with much reason the apple of the Head's eye and became head of his house. He was going to Cambridge and was being groomed by the Head for the Church when the war broke out. He was one of those young men whose loss in the war deprived the country of the best of its leaders."

The collection of poems in Mark's diary reveals other facets of his nature, his extreme romanticism, his love of the exotic, his introspection. The influences upon him were varied. As well as Kipling, he admired Robert Louis Stevenson, and the latter's collection *A Child's Garden of Verses and Underwoods*, featured twice in his collection of quotations. "It is not yours, O Mother to complain" was the first excerpt:

Mark Hill, centre, seated, with his group of house prefects, 1912. George Fenchelle, Henry Russell and Neill Newsum, all killed in the war, are grouped as a trio standing behind Hill.

"So like a sword the son shall roam
On nobler missions sent, –
And as the smith remained at home
In peaceful turret pent
So sits the while at home, the mother, well content."

Mark Hill also derived some lines and titles from Horace's *Odes*, from *Bush Ballads and Galloping Rhymes* by Adam Lindsay Gordon, from John Bunyan and from a sermon by John Wesley. His own poems were escapist and romantic, often retreating into a mythological world. He wrote of pyramids, Egyptian gods and goddesses, of eastern gardens. But his inner thoughts reflected upon dreams and the nature of dreaming, of the place of man in the infinity of space and time, of the significance of individual life. Often his shorter poems on such themes were his most successful, as in *The Mists of Sleep*:

"As the Mists of Sleep crept over me
Sealing my eyelids with soft kisses
The consciousness of this world
Vanished away
And darkness surrounded me."

After Mark's death, Mrs Hill received, rather unusually, a letter from Mark's servant, Private F. Drakeford, who tried hard and touchingly to comfort her on the loss of the second of her three sons:

> "No doubt you have heard from the War Office before now, but I thought it was only right that I should write a line to you, to let you know what a gallant death he met. I was servant to your son from when he came out again after being wounded [*in October 1915*], and I am glad to say I was getting along very nice before this big attack, and I can assure you it came as a big blow to me when he was killed. Dear Mrs Hill, I am sorry I could not write to you before, but we have been so busy since the morning we made the attack so I hope you won't mind, it was a big hit for us, but we did all that we were asked to do. All our Officers were killed or wounded before nightfall, so you can guess we had a hard task before us. I know how hard it must be for you, but perhaps it will be some relief for you to know that He suffered no pain, the Germans were just making a counter attack after we had taken the village, and your Son was in charge of what men were left, he was very Brave and I am sure he could see no danger, all of a sudden a machine-gun opened fire on us, and it was then that He met His death, but not before he had done some splendid work. Dear Mrs Hill I managed to get through alright, but I never thought anyone would get away at one time, it was awfull while it lasted. I think we lost about one half of our Battalion, either killed wounded or missing. It will be a big relief when this terrible lot is over, and those that are left can get back again to the Dear Ones we have left behind. Of course a great many will never see Home again, but all we can do is to cheer up and Hope for the Best. I hope by now you have received all His Clothes and other kit, I think they were sent off yesterday. Dear Mrs Hill I must close my short letter now, hoping these few lines will help to Cheer you, if it is only a little, and as I have said before, you have every reason to be Proud of your Son, for no man could meet a more Glorious Death than He did, being killed while upholding the Honour of His Regiment."

The Commonwealth War Graves Commission records of soldiers who fell in the First World War include no reference to an F. Drakeford, so it is to be hoped that he, at least, returned to his "Dear Ones".

As for Mark, perhaps his own words should be his epitaph:

> "We are but dust and shadow, we who dwell
> Within the world of changing dust and shade:
> And comes the question – wherefore were we made?
> Wherefore was it created? Who can tell?
> That we, though others fail, made stand alone
> The steadfast banner of our faith unfurled;
> To send some flash of light across the world,
> Ere we pass back into the great unknown."

Nearly 50 letters of Cuthbert Hill's friend Alleyne Boxall, written home to his mother between mid-1916 and the end of the war, survive. They form an archive which reveals a life in some ways and at some times very much of the sort he might have had in a peacetime university setting, but with the danger and risk of injury or death – rarely spoken of but ever-present – forming a grim backdrop. Alleyne met friends, dined and drank with them, played cards and had fun, but the news of his friends he sent home was usually the news of their deaths. Boxall, as so many others did, wrote home about those things that would not cause anxiety, in his case to a widowed mother. For the most part he concentrated in his letters on the brighter moments, on the important matters of food and drink, on letters and news to and from Gresham's. Apart from sparing the feelings of relatives, it was important in maintaining a soldier's sanity that he did not dwell all the time on the grim scenes of the trenches. In his first surviving letter, written on 9 June 1916, about two weeks after his arrival in France with the 2nd Battalion York and Lancaster Regiment, Alleyne spoke of "some quite narrow enough shaves. We live like rats in a cave!!!... I am very busy censoring letters at present."

The following day it had rained:

> "I have been steadily scraping mud off my clothes since early this morning and it is now nearly tea time... We get nearly as good food to eat as we do in England, certainly better than we did at Etaples [*at the universally-hated training centre*]. I am quite enjoying myself."

Several days later, food was again a topic of his letter home.

> "I have a very good cook and so have excellent meals together with Port Wine and Whiskey. So provided the old German keeps quiet I

> ought to have an exceedingly enjoyable time. I have a dugout to myself."

So far so good, but the following month the story was not quite the same. In a letter which began with thanks for "the parcel containing the cake, artichokes, cheese, tinned fruit and sweets", he moved to:

> "Aren't there a tremendous number of York and Lancasters in the casualty list nowadays? You might get me an identity disc, silver, for the wrist. I have only a cardboard one. Have on it '2nd Lt. H. A. Boxall. York and Lancaster Regiment. C of E.'"

Two days later:

> "Do you remember Fenchelle or Russell at Holt? Both have been killed and Barker wounded."

The Roll of Guns His Requiem

GEORGE Fenchelle had been killed on 30 June while serving with the Sussex Regiment, east of Richebourg l'Avoue. Not only was he a friend of Boxall but he was also one of Cuthbert Hill's fellow actors and team-mates at Gresham's. In the summer of 1913 both Hill brothers, Fenchelle, Frank Halsey and David Jacques had taken major roles in the annual Shakespearean play performed in the school's outdoor theatre in the woods, a rural amphitheatre dugout of a slight hillside and terraced by the schoolboys of 1907. It was perhaps an unusual choice of play, by no means the most popular of Shakespeare's comedies, *Love's Labour's Lost.* With hindsight many references in the last act seem resonant: the King, played by Mark Hill, says:

> "If this, or more than this, I would deny
> To flatter up these powers of mine with rest,
> The sudden hand of death close up my eye!"
> Berowne (Frank Halsey) asks Rosaline (Cuthbert Hill) to impose a service on him so that he might win her love.
> She answers:
> "You shall this twelvemonth term from day to day
> Visit the speechless sick, and still converse
> With groaning wretches; and your task shall be
> With all the fierce endeavour of your wit
> To enforce the pained impotent to smile."
> His rejoinder is:
> "To move wild laughter in the throat of death?
> It cannot be; it is impossible;
> Mirth cannot move a soul in agony."

The King and his three lords in Shakespeare's *Love's Labour's Lost*, performed in the school's theatre in the woods in summer 1913. Behind the table, from left to right: Frank Halsey, George Fenchelle, Mark Hill and David Jacques. All four lost their lives in the war.

The play's central characters are a group of young lords, comrades. In this fateful production the King of Navarre, all his three lords, Rosaline, and the princess's page, Alfred Hyde, then aged only 14, lost their lives in the war.

The last scene contains lines which, in the context of what was to come, were charged with deep meaning. The central concern is with death and mourning, and almost the last lines of the play are given to Ver, Spring, and Hiems, Winter. It is Winter who speaks of the icicles which hang by the wall, the wind that blows, the coughing, snow, and raw noses of that season. Armado, the Spaniard, ends the play. "The words of Mercury are hard after the songs of Apollo. You that way; we this way."

The symbolism seems inescapable.

As well as an actor, George Fenchelle had been one of the small group of school prefects, a good games player, and a member of the OTC band. His life was, of course, short – he was only 21 when he died – but he had travelled to Russia where he had worked in a business house in St Petersburg, an interesting experience no doubt in those last days before the Russian Revolution. During the war he had spent some time with the Intelligence Corps. The details of his death are few. A fellow soldier described his leading an advance at 3.30am: "We reached the German front line trenches and then I saw the lieutenant hit, and fall. I didn't see him again." The German government wrote to the War Office to say that they had Fenchelle's effects. All they had, in fact, was his identity disc, which was duly returned. The rest of his possessions were lost in the chaos of war.

Predictably, the great offensive on the Somme claimed its share of Greshamians. The month of July alone brought seven fatalities, mostly from battles on the Somme. Two fell amongst the total of 20,000 on the notorious first day, 1 July. That day – which according to John Keegan saw "the greatest loss of life in British military history" – Henry Scott-Holmes, a second-lieutenant of the Norfolk Division of the Royal Engineers, died, "leading his men in the face of heavy fire". It is not possible to quantify the ill effects of the death of a son, but "Sonny's" death left his family bereft materially as well as emotionally.

His father's profession on Henry's birth certificate was given as "Gentleman". His means had ebbed, his son had been withdrawn from Gresham's and Henry's mother was reduced after the death of her son to ask for, as she termed it, "a mother's pension", as Henry had been supporting his family financially on a regular basis. Walter Gissing, a rifleman with the Queen's Westminster Rifles, also lost his life on 1 July. In the overwhelming task of bringing in the wounded and the dead in the days following, neither was to be rewarded with a known grave, and both names are to be found on the Thiepval Memorial. One letter to *The Gresham*, from Cyril Masterman, a second-lieutenant in the Hampshire Regiment, refers to that awful day, 1 July:

> "The trenches up here are very wet in parts, well above the knees in liquid mud, and have also been knocked about a good deal from the show on 1 July. I was not in that myself, I am sorry to say, but with another soldier was kept back in reserve. Our regiment did very good work, but suffered heavy casualties. I cannot say very much about the business, but I think the papers will probably mention us again for tough work. The Corps Commander came up two days after the push to speak to the battalion himself. Our losses in officers have been especially heavy, and I think there must have been special snipers told off for the job. I am at present commanding a company, as we are so short. The wounded are still coming in from no man's land even now. One came in the night before last having been out ten days. He was hit in four places, but

> his wounds were healing well and he seemed quite cheery. Apparently he had been living on the rations of those killed out there. It is almost incredible that he should have lived through it, as both sides pump shells into No Man's Land hard daily. It seems terrible to think of the wounded lying out so long, but it is impossible to find them all there."

On 7 July, Geoffrey Barratt, a second-lieutenant with the Lancashire Fusiliers, fell in action, unwittingly providing an example from Gresham's of those who were wounded then lost in the maelstrom of battle. The details of his fate were never known to those at Gresham's, the only information reaching the school being that he was:

> "...buried by a shell when some others were killed. When he was got out he was found to be unconscious. The particular spot where this happened had to be abandoned; since then nothing has been heard of him."

This bare account conceals a great deal. His service record includes a page headed "For information only. Not to be communicated outside the War Office." Beneath is an extraordinary story of the investigation into Barratt's death. It is peppered with misspellings of Barratt's name and inaccurate dating of events. Private S. Cattell of the 5th Worcester Regiment made several statements, the first of which described how Cattell had been told to bury Barratt, and on doing so found some photographs which he sent to the *News Of The World* for publication. These were identified by Geoffrey's mother as being of her son. His father was confused. Where were his son's identity disc and letters? He persisted in his enquiries, but was finally told on 24 March 1917 that there was no reason to believe that the statement of Private Cattell was incorrect. But perhaps there was. On the same page as Cattell's first statement is a memorandum crossed through strongly by the War Office with a clear black line. It reads thus:

> "Private Mitchell states that 2nd Lt. G. R. V. Barratt had just ordered him to lead on and that having proceeded about 15 yards he saw a large shell explode close to this officer and blow him completely to pieces."

That was just as likely to be true as any other account, but this unspeakably dreadful version, understandably, could not be conveyed to Barratt's family.

Henry Russell, whose death was noted by Alleyne Boxall, had survived the horrors of the Gallipoli campaign, and service in Egypt, but was severely wounded by a shell on 11 July while serving as a lieutenant with the Essex Regiment. He died in hospital at Gezaincourt the same day. The son of an Essex landowner and farmer, he had gone up to New College, Oxford, to read Science Mechanics and Physics in early 1914. His application for a temporary commission was signed by his headmaster, who affirmed his good character, and by the legendary warden of New College, W. A. Spooner (famous for his Spoonerisms) who confirmed his good educational standard. In academic terms, though, Russell, like several other Greshamians at university, was struggling to make the grade. Twice he failed his preliminary exams in his additional subject and once in Maths. It is perhaps a timely reminder in what might seem to be a chronicle of bravery and glittering achievement that these young men were human enough to fail, at least in some respects, not always covering themselves in academic as well as military glory. During his time in France, Russell wrote two letters back to school, the first describing the huge size of the field guns and their capacity to inflict damage:

> "Two fields away from my billet is a -inch gun on a fixed concrete base, worked by electricity from a power station set up in the field for it. The shells are just under a ton in weight and are worked and lifted by cranes. The whole thing, of course, is worked by a system of wireless from our aeroplane observer, and yesterday it shelled a town 9 and a half miles away." (Russell did not specify what size the gun was.)

His second letter revealed the seriousness of the situation in his battalion.

> "The other day our battalion went into action about 750 men and 23 officers strong and came out with about 110 men and 1 officer; all our best men and officers have gone and we shall never be able to replace them, I am sorry to say, as our reinforcements are very young and small. Thus I find myself second in command of the battalion and over a company of 26 fighting strength; so as you can guess, there is plenty of work to be done."

Russell speaks of the youth of the new recruits, but it is worth noting that he himself was only 21 when he died.

Laurence Biden, serving as a lieutenant with the Royal Warwickshire

Regiment, was severely wounded at Bazentin on 14 July, on the same day and in the same action in which Mark Hill was killed. He never recovered from his injuries and died over a year later in Brighton after an operation in October 1917.

On 16 July, Dawson Atkin – he of the wry humour – died of wounds after the bloodbath of High Wood, described by a soldier contemporary as "a horrible, terrible massacre". The military historian Richard Holmes in his book *The Western Front* has described High Wood as "ghastly by day, ghostly by night, the rottenest place on the Somme". On the 15th, Atkin, with thousands of others, suffered the barrage of machine-gun, sniper fire and shells from an enemy concealed but very much undefeated, while working to dig trenches to "consolidate the line" among the tangle of tree roots and fallen branches to which High Wood had been reduced. These trenches were abandoned the following day. The news that reached school was that Atkin:

> "...was trying to make better cover by connecting up a number of shell holes with trenches, and it was while attempting this work that he was hit by shrapnel in several places. His men wanted to carry him back, but as this meant their going over the open he would not let them. He walked some way, but had to give in and was carried the remainder of the distance. It is probable that the head wounds caused concussion, from which he died about 30 hours later. We have heard from many how devoted his men were to him. Though he was so strict and determined to have his team smart (it was second only to an Indian one) he was more like a brother than an officer; he gave nearly his whole time to them and was always teaching them, always trying to make them keen on their work. One man said, 'We would far rather be in the trenches with Mr Atkin than in billets.'"

Concern was being expressed about John Foster, who had been reported missing on 23 July. It was known that he had been hit by a bullet above the eye while leading his platoon. Apparently two of his men dressed his wound and bandaged him, then lifted him into a shell hole, but when afterwards a search party went out to bring him in, he was not to be found. The hope was that the Germans had captured him. Some months later he was reported "killed", but it seems that his father would not give up hope that he was alive. It was not until *The Gresham* of February 1917 that his death was reported. "...there is no doubt now that he died of wounds on 23 July." Rather unusually for a Greshamian, Foster started in the ranks. His captain later wrote:

> "He was far and away the best officer in the regiment; his having served in the ranks and his six months' experience at the Front made him a steady leader. He had splendid command of his men, knew no fear and was the life and soul of the crowd."

It is interesting to see that by this stage of the war, rankers were being promoted to officers' roles. Often, as in this case, they made the transition very well once they had gained the habit of authority, and proved to be very successful leaders.

The month of July ended as it had begun. Douglas Richardson, a captain in the Royal Flying Corps, was killed on the 29th. He had studied engineering at the Liverpool Institute and had joined the Cheshire Field Company, Royal Engineers in 1913. Thus he was in camp when war was declared. In November 1914 he went out to France, writing a most informative letter home at that time:

> "Where we are at present we have 1,200 yards of open country to cross before we get to the trenches, which are situated in a very shallow valley; the result is we get all the 'overs' ('overs' are shots which go high and are the general rule at night). The result is I am always quite glad to get into a trench. One still talks about getting 'into' a trench, though there is nothing much to get into except the eternal mud – the trenches consisting of a parapet about four feet high in most cases. On fine nights one can generally keep fairly clean, but when it is dark it is nearly impossible to miss the 'crump' (shell) holes, which are full of water.
> Please do not think, though, that a sapper is only supposed to work, for it was two field companies that made the bayonet charge when the Prussian Guard had broken the line and who saved us from goodness knows what."

In May 1915 he was invalided home suffering from pleurisy. His family records recount that it was at this time when he was at home ill that he received the insult of a bunch of white feathers, a conventional accusation of cowardice at the time, "from someone who should have known better". Later, Richardson joined the RFC, gaining his wings in February 1916. In France from March, he had won promotion to captain and flight commander with the 29th Squadron on his 24th birthday on 22 June, only the month before he was killed while flying an FE8 near Ypres.

On the same day that Richardson died, 29 July, at Gresham's it was Speech Day. By now 30 Greshamians had been killed and they were much on Howson's mind. The headmaster began by speaking of the Old Boys:

> "Late in 1914 and still more so in 1915, many of us felt confident that today we should see such a rally of Old Boys as was never before seen at Holt, but now we must wait till 1917. In the meantime they are seldom out of our thoughts. It is difficult to speak of those who will never come, for words cannot be a measure of sorrow. We are deeply conscious of their gallant sacrifice and of our incalculable loss."

He was proud to mention:

> "Twice I have received gratifying tributes indicating the high esteem in which the War Office hold officers who have come from this school."

Most of the boys seated in the room that year were too young to see much active service, but one prize-winner, for German, Alfred Hyde, was to meet his death in the air just two months before the war ended.

The Somme Offensive continued throughout the summer and into the autumn. On 2 September, Cosmo Duff-Gordon joined the number who fell in one of "the bloody struggles for tiny patches of ground" (Keegan) – in his case at Guillemont "while leading his men [*a machine-gun team*] into action." Like so many others, Duff-Gordon was exposed to danger while helping another man:

> "One of the team was wounded and your son stayed and bandaged him up. After this he took the tripod which the wounded man had been carrying, and was just starting to carry it himself when he was hit."

One of the school's most local boys, Archer Neal, who came from Holt itself, was killed only days later. He was one of the few Greshamians to win a Military Medal, as he was not an officer. He met his death on 15 September in the "great Guards' attack at Ginchy" and was buried in Delville Wood, near his former schoolfellow, Cosmo Duff-Gordon. A letter written to his brother reveals that Archer:

> "...received his medal for showing great coolness under very heavy 'minenwerfer' (trench mortar) fire in the Ypres Salient when the platoon was isolated... No one saw him actually hit, but he was found dead. He was an extremely good soldier and his loss was much felt by all."

On the same page of the school magazine which reported Duff-Gordon's death, appear three gazette entries of young men who had been awarded the Military Cross. This decoration was brought into being early in the war, in December 1914, and Gresham's men won a good number of them. Of these, Estcourt and Graves were to die later in the war. But in the summer of 1916, Adrian Graves, the younger brother of the imprisoned Cecil, was fulfilling all his schoolboy promise. A letter from him in the same edition describes his feelings about the "push" and he was in buoyant mood:

> "Everyone is very confident about the success of the push. We have got the ascendancy over the German in munitions – here at least, and are getting it in men."

He described an incident of three weeks before:

> "Some way to our left we could see a long string of Germans without arms and equipment coming down a communication trench towards our lines. Some of our bombers had found them weeping and crying 'Merci Kamerad' – they actually wept! And then the German artillery began to shell them with shrapnel, and the prisoners did not waste much time in coming over. As they passed us they looked a very unhappy crowd. The men kept on muttering 'Krieg ist nicht gut,' while others seemed rather pleased to be out of it."

Months later, descriptions of the Somme battle were still filtering through to school. George Hawksley was once again at the Front after his spell in hospital in England suffering from "debility". It seems unlikely that the dictionary definition of debility, "tired and weak", is accurate in this case. Presumably most soldiers on the Western Front were tired by 1916, but they were not all being sent home. More likely is that the sensitive Hawksley had suffered some sort of emotional crisis or even a breakdown. In terms of what he had witnessed, and his moving response to such scenes, it would not be surprising. He wrote of the sight which greeted him on a fine summer evening, 10 July, between Crucifix Corner, so lethal to the Devonshires, and La Boisselle to the north:

> "...as one topped the ridge a splendid and awful sight presented itself. For miles, as far as the eye could see, there stretched a countryside so blasted and scoured that no native could have recognised it. Mile upon mile, acre upon acre, of captured trenches sprawled white and battered. Beneath was La Boisselle, a few stumps of trees and mounds of bricks. To the left over the skyline the shells were spraying Contalmaison and Pozières; and in the foreground, in front of our old lines of squalid trenches, was a ghastly No Man's Land, simply thick with our dead – English, Scotch, Irish and Welsh – they lay in lines and clumps, one of the most pitiful sights I ever saw."

Hawksley's letter confirms that of Masterman, except that the wounded who had not been brought in had by this time died, of course. Ten days after the beginning of the "Big Push" the bodies of the dead had by no means all been recovered. Several contemporary accounts speak of the numbers of blackening corpses lying just yards in front of the trench from which they had climbed, on what was for many of the members of Kitchener's army, their first sortie "over the top".

As the dreadful year of 1916 drew towards its end, the casualties kept on coming. Charles Shepherd and Humphrey Thorn, both in the 7th Battalion of the Norfolk Regiment, both second-lieutenants, fell on the same day in the same action, and died within 24 hours of one another, Shepherd on 12 October and Thorn on the 13th. Shortly before, Thorn had been moved to express his views and feelings in a letter to *The Gresham*. His attitude to the enemy is not an isolated one. Many British soldiers had come to acknowledge the courage and soldierly qualities of the Germans:

> "I have heard people run the German down as a soldier, but personally I think he is by no means to be despised. Considering the forces he has had to face he has stuck it awfully well. He shelled us badly, but it was nothing to what our guns gave him. Proper trenches anywhere near the front line are non-existent, they are simply connected shell holes. The sight of some of the ruined French towns makes one realise what one is really fighting for. I think they ought to bring some of the 'conscientious objectors' out and show them things. Nobody likes war, but anyone who calls himself British would, I am sure, rather join the army than see English towns like some of these."

Thorn was wounded in the thigh and the abdomen, the latter proving fatal, as was so often the case in that war. Such soft tissue damage was particularly vulnerable to infection and required delicate and complicated surgery not possible in the primitive medical circumstances. One of Humphrey Thorn's fellow officers wrote to Mr Thorn after Humphrey's death:

> "Your son, as you will have heard from the Colonel, was mortally wounded on the 12th, the day before yesterday, and died last night at the casualty clearing station. I wish I could give you some comfort. All I can say is that your son died magnificently in the assault on the enemy's front line. He was hit by machine-gun bullets. I daresay you have heard of Shepherd, who was also at Gresham's. He too was killed, on the 12th, shot through the head. Your son was a great favourite and a capable officer."

About a week later, on 21 October, Stanley Marriott of the Royal Engineers was killed by the explosion of a shell while in charge of a working party of 600 infantry digging a trench late in the evening. He was talking to a fellow officer when a heavy shell killed them both instantly. Shellfire was the source of the greatest number of casualties in the war. It is estimated that three quarters of all wounds were inflicted by shells, which could and often did, blow men to pieces. Suspiciously, many of the Gresham's men died instantly or with a single shot. A clean death was seen as the kindest way to describe to relatives the end of a loved son or husband, as Geoffrey Barratt's case testifies. The alternative was simply too grotesque. It is therefore impossible to know how many of the men actually died in the manner described in their tributes. Marriott is commemorated on a special memorial in the Guards' Cemetery at Lesboeufs, because no one is sure of his exact resting-place. The third of seven sons, Stanley Marriott, known to his family as "Todd", was thought by his parents to be the cleverest of all the boys. His father, who had played an important part in the building of the railway so important to North Norfolk communications in the early 20th century, had hoped that Todd would be his successor in that work. Instead, after their son's death the family moved away from their home in Brinton, only a few miles from Holt, and went to Sheringham, to try to begin again in a new place. Until the end of her life, Todd's mother wore a locket containing his photograph.

Away from the trenches, Edward Giles met his death as a result of an accident while he was flying a new plane from Filton Aerodrome near Bristol, where he was stationed, to Farnborough. He got lost in fog and, not realising the nature of the country, flew into a hill only about 15 miles from Bristol. He was killed instantly. He had started his military service as workshop officer to the Indian Cavalry Corps in France, but felt that this was too comfortable. Accepted by the RFC in January 1916, he eventually achieved his ambition to become a pilot. An unwise flight in difficult November conditions was to prove a challenge too far. His housemaster, J. R. Eccles, wrote of him:

> "…he was one of the best boy engineers the school has known… he was one of those delightful natures who radiate kindness, and he did so without a trace of self-consciousness… He had a simple, joyous innocent nature, which won him a host of friends."

On the same day that Edward Giles was being buried in Canford Cemetery, Vivian Smith died in action in France while serving as a captain in the Wiltshire Regiment. He was the only member of the school's staff employed at Gresham's in 1914 who was to die in the war, although another master at the school, between 1911 and 1912, Geoffrey Day, also lost his life in France, on the Somme. Smith was deeply mourned by those who had known him at school and a vivid picture emerges of the handsome young art master who had been popular with the boys. The editor of *The Gresham* waxed too lyrical for modern taste:

> "We cannot yet write what he was to us and what we owed to him; the blow is too recent and our souls are numb. In the distant quieter days, when with less pain we can appraise our dead, those who knew and loved him will share many a precious memory. And on the wind-swept wastes by Salthouse, in the villages that ring us, where the children loved him and many a homely cottager will mourn him, there will the past live and there shall we meet him again, *qui ante diem periit, sed miles, sed pro patria.*"

Vivian Smith.

The last words echo those made famous by another First World War soldier, and casualty, Wilfred Owen, in his poem *Dulce et Decorum Est.* It is significant that at Gresham's as late as December 1916 they could be quoted without a trace of the savage irony which permeates Owen's poem.

The accounts from the Front of Smith's death were

more direct, although not necessarily accurate. The letter from the colonel of the regiment to Smith's father bears all the marks of an oft-repeated list of clichés, particularly when set against the tributes of those who knew Smith better, although his bravery is not in doubt:

> "He was a remarkably brave man, an extremely good soldier and a natural leader of men. Personally he was of the greatest assistance to me, always cheery, thoroughly to be relied upon on all occasions, no matter how trying they were, making light of difficulties, taking great care of his men and never sparing himself to look after them. I deplore his loss more than I can say. He was killed, as you probably know, when binding another man's wound. We carried his body and buried him in the cemetery back behind the lines. His grave is marked."

A fellow officer of Vivian Smith also wrote of his burial, a scene which could well have inspired one of Smith's paintings:

> "He went to tie up a wounded man and a shell landed in the trench and he was killed instantly. We got him out yesterday and buried him in the cemetery at Aveluy. A wooden cross is being put up on the grave. I went to the funeral service last night. The cemetery is on the side of a slight hill below the village. We buried him with the ruined church and the sunset as a background and the roll of guns his requiem. I cannot say how sorry I feel."

The wooden cross has been replaced by Portland stone, but in other respects the scene is utterly recognisable today.

Vivian Smith had been a pupil at Sherborne School and afterwards had specialised in the study of animal painting. He came to Gresham's in 1907 as drawing master and exhibited his work several times at the Royal Academy. A signed oil painting by him exists today in Holt. Entitled *Mr Jex's Pigeon*, it commemorates a flight by this remarkable bird to France. An Old Boy of Gresham's wrote of him:

> "He portrayed horses with a sympathy and understanding that few could equal... He loved great gloomy stables and the vastness of cathedrals in the evening time... He was not concerned with the actual progress of work, but with the rest that comes after work. Such pictures as 'The Day's Work Done' and 'Under the Hawthorn

> Tree', will explain what I mean. Through the tranquillity of the scenes we are forced to recognise the toil of the day that preceded the rest of the evening. It was his expression of the yearning for that peace in life which he was destined to attain only in death."

In contrast to this romantic and tragic image, a boy still at Gresham's wrote of his former teacher: "We can never forget his merry tea-parties at Hanworth House." A colleague wrote a feeling and personal obituary to him in the school magazine echoing that same image, speaking of him as "the best and merriest of companions by the fireside," yet:

> "...I see him most plainly strolling from net to net in the summer evenings, leading the scrum in that old blue-and-white jersey, striding down to Salthouse by moonlight, walking through his beloved Dorset, or on the northern fells which he came to know and love only in the last years of his life."

Several months after Smith's death, a Lieutenant-Colonel Shephard, who had served with him between November 1914 and September 1915, gave an inkling of the personal difficulty war presented to him. After commending his work in training picked men to sketch the trenches, and for his own silhouette sketches, Shephard commented:

> "All the more credit is due to him for his consistent good work and spirits from the fact that owing to his highly strung and artistic temperament the many sordid scenes of ruin and the rough life of warfare were most uncongenial to him."

His personal achievement was considerable: he was mentioned in despatches from General Sir Douglas Haig on 13 November, the day he was killed: "For gallant and distinguished service in the Field."

The year ended with the deaths on the Somme of Noel Barker of the Dorsetshire Regiment (not related to the three Barker brothers) on 19 November, and in northern France of David Jacques, aged only 19, on 1 December. Barker's death during the Battle of the Ancre was described thus:

> "It happened about 4pm. It was the day following the attack, when we were subjected to a most fierce bombardment the whole of the

> day, but we were safe in the dugouts. When a lull took place, Barker went out fearlessly to see what damage had been done, when a shell fell in the trench, killing him instantly. His loss was a real blow to me as we have been such close companions for the past year. He was cheerful and energetic to the last, and never once did I hear him complain, and things have been very rough out here this last two months."

Second-Lieutenant David Jacques of The Queen's (Royal West Surrey Regiment) fell to a sniper, as had Marlborough Crosse. It seems that he had taken a rifle to try to shoot the sniper who was firing on his men, but himself died with a bullet to the head without regaining consciousness, or so it was said. Perhaps he had been influenced by Vivian Smith, but at any rate Jacques' housemaster, Mr Eccles, wrote of him:

> "He could draw animals with no little skill, and was at one time thinking of devoting himself to art, but he felt called to prepare for Holy Orders. He was a fine character, with a just appreciation of the things that count in life. He had a fine physique. It was a delight to see him taking the hurdles and to watch him running after the ball in the 'deep field' and throwing it in. But it is that attractive and winning personality which one will never forget."

In David Jacques' service record is preserved a sad letter from his father. "Amongst my son's possessions was a letter to his mother," he wrote. The letter had been sent to the War Office, perhaps for censoring, guessed Jacques' father, but now any content relating to the war was not relevant, as weeks had passed. Mr Jacques requested the letter, "for my wife as it is of course of very great value to her now." It is good to know that the letter was sent to Mrs Jacques, unopened by the censor.

The five-month Battle of the Somme was won by the British at an unspeakable cost of lives, the memory of which echoed through the 20th century. Such losses led to a change of battle tactics in 1917 as such casualty lists provoked universal horror and revulsion. The keynote of the year was sacrifice, for Gresham's as well as the nation: between July and November, Howson had lost 18 of his "boys".

Flights, Fights and Falls

THE "last" Christmas of the war, as so many hoped the Christmas of 1916 would be, ushered in a period of intense cold in North Norfolk, the minimum temperature recorded for 1916 being 20 degrees Fahrenheit. One night in early 1917, however, 34 degrees of frost was recorded. Hard frosts and snow led to divided allegiances at school, with some boys favouring skating and others tobogganing. Howson, for his part, was a keen skater and frequently lent his boots and skates to boys who wanted to have a go. The ground outside the chapel had been levelled and the plan was to plant it with potatoes, as part of the war effort. The potatoes contributed to the feeding of several of the houses. For the record, the south side did very well, the north side poorly. The debt on the chapel building was not yet paid off, so it was not possible to begin the panelling which would conceal the whitewashed walls and the radiators. "School Notes" in *The Gresham* records: "The big explosion on Friday 19 January 1917 was heard quite distinctly about 7.03pm at the school. This was, as far as one could ascertain, almost exactly ten minutes after its occurrence." In such ways the war was extraordinarily close.

The winter of 1916-17 proved to be the coldest for 30 years, and the weather that caused excitement and fun at Gresham's produced desperately hard conditions for those in the trenches of France and Flanders. In London when there was one degree of frost, there was a reading of 15 degrees in Arras. For the first two months of the year, mercifully, the accounts of Greshamian deaths at the Front ceased, but in March the dismal list was lengthened with the news that Leon Soman had died in Baghdad on the 9th. He had begun his war serving with the Canadian Expeditionary Force but at the time of his death he was involved in a frustrating attempt by the North Lancashire battalion, for which he was acting as adjutant, to get supplies and ammunition across the River Dialah under cover of darkness. Soman had been chosen to pay out the rope to a swimmer, but seeing that the line:

"...had got entangled in a bush at the water's edge, he ran forward to free it, and whilst doing so he was silhouetted against the bank by the light of the moon, and a moment later was shot through the heart by a sniper and died almost immediately, without being able to utter a word."

He was buried where he fell on the left bank of the river, a grave that was of course subsequently lost, and Soman is today commemorated on the Basra Memorial. It seems particularly mean-spirited that the Canadian government took the trouble after Soman's death to recover an overpayment of 7s 1d (about 35p) from his estate. He, on the other hand, had asked that in the event of his death, a cheque for 20 guineas (£21) should be sent to school as a contribution to the Old Boys' Chapel Fund.

John Warwick, a major with the Oxford and Bucks Light Infantry, had been killed on 10 March by a gas shell bursting in the entrance to his dugout.

A week later, Frederick Walker, aged only 18, became the second of Gresham's 15 airmen to die, and a steady trickle of reports for the roll of honour began once again. Walker was probably a victim of the inadequate training received by pilots in the spring of 1917. It was not for nothing that the April of that year was called "Bloody April." He took off, climbed, the engine stalled and his machine hit the ground in a spinning nose-dive in which he was, of course, killed immediately. He was not the only OG to meet his death in such a way.

One survivor of the war, Robert Fitzgerald (who appears on the 1914 cricket photograph) wrote to school a powerful and atmospheric account of the successful assault on Vimy Ridge in April 1917 by British and Canadian troops:

"The preliminary bombardment started four days before the actual show, a steady shelling all day and night. We did not hear much of this as we were billeted in some gigantic caves capable of holding 6,000 men. Well, we were in the caves until 9 o'clock on Sunday night. That night we all moved up to the assembly trenches, and there we had a cold and dreary vigil until half-past five on Monday morning, the 9th. We only suffered one casualty in these 'jumping off' trenches, in spite of short bursts of shelling from his 'whizz-bang' batteries.

At three o'clock it began to rain pretty heavily, which made things most unpleasant; at five o'clock we all partook of our last meal before going over, and my Company Commander and myself consumed two hard-boiled eggs in stony silence. At 5.30 am the

Canadians went over the top in front of Vimy Ridge, preceded by an intense barrage from our Field Guns, and also a liquid fire attack, the most wonderful sight you can possibly imagine.

From where we were in our trenches we could see the Vimy Ridge quite plainly, and, on the stroke of 5.30, two mines went up, which was the signal for our guns to open fire and at the same time let off liquid fire. The Bosche at once sent up every conceivable coloured rocket and alarm signals, green stars, red rockets, lovely golden rain star shells, in fact an exact imitation of a Brock's firework display. This attack took place two hours before ours, which started at 7.34 am. The idea was to make him think that our attack was only going to be a feint one, and not on a big scale, and also to deceive him into thinking that our attack would not come off the same day as the Vimy Ridge show.

At 7.34am we went over behind our barrage followed by four tanks. For the first 200 yards the going was uphill, and by the time we reached the summit of the Ridge there was not an ounce of wind left in any of the men to do the remaining 300 yards, and we were also rather disorganised. On coming in sight of the Bosche we were met by machine-gun fire and a certain amount of rifle fire, but not much shelling. At one moment things looked rather black, as we came up to our barrage too soon and were compelled to halt for a couple of minutes, during which time we took cover as best we could in shell holes, from which we had a good deal of trouble in getting the men out as soon as the barrage lifted, but we managed to reach our objective, where the Bosche was very ready to give himself up.

The trenches were wiped out of existence, and not a trace of wire, which bears testimony to the marvellous shooting of the Artillery. They came streaming out of their dugouts by the hundreds, miserable wretches, having been down there without food for the previous two days; in fact an officer came out of a dugout after we had been there a couple of hours, calmly smoking a cigar, and was very much astonished to find British Tommies in possession of his sector of the trench. This same officer, seeing an officer in our Company walking towards him, shot him point blank, killing him instantly, and then had the cheek to hold up his hands in surrender. He did not hold them up for long though, being shot dead by the officer's servant. I have related this small incident

> just to show the true character of the Bosche officers. They are simply out to kill, and when they have done that they are satisfied."

By this time, thanks to 'the submarine menace', rationing had become part of school life at Gresham's. The boys were on their honour not to eat more than four and a half rounds of bread a day, to be divided, according to individual choice, between breakfast and tea. For supper, they had a slice of bread "with an average of three currants in it", and cold rice was sometimes substituted for potatoes at lunch. Water was in short supply, and in the circumstances the boys decided to give up showering in the mornings as it was dispiriting to stand under a mere trickle of cold water. When this dereliction of duty was discovered by the matron and reported to Wynne Willson he:

> "...in a long lecture expressed his disgust at our dirty, un-Scoutlike and effeminate ways – 'I suppose you will be wanting hot water bottles next!' Little did he know the awful truth – several boys were already using their khaki Boy Scout water-bottles for that purpose, furtively filling them from the hot tap before going to bed."

In the spring of 1917, Howson's health failed and he was ill for some months. In early May, his younger sister Mary, known to the boys of Gresham's as "Matron", wrote a card to Alleyne Boxall, followed by a letter from Howson himself later in the month. In it he commented that he was still not well but hoped to be back at school by half-term. By early June he had not been able to return to work, and even in July he was still not fully recovered. On Speech Day, 27 July, he made what he described as a "five-minute speech" (and it *was* short) in which he referred to the kindness and help he had received, but his last words were for his boys:

> "I am sure you will join me in the earnest wish for a speedy end of this war, and a safe return for the Old Boys who are so much in our thoughts."

Sir Edward Busk was encouraged that the headmaster was so much recovered, and hoped that the holiday would bring further improvement in his health, which apparently was the case. He pointed out that the table was bare of prizes, explaining that it was both difficult to obtain the necessary bookbinders or indeed the leather for the books, so the order was given for the booksellers to produce the required book prizes within six months. The guest of honour was the Dean of Norwich, Dr Beeching, who quoted a remark from Ian Hay, then a distinguished army officer but after the war better known for his light novels and plays. Hay had said in *The Times* that the war was "being won by the second-lieutenants" – that is, by the public schools. In later, more egalitarian times, that view would cause outrage, but it is interesting that it was made at the time.

By July, of course, several more second-lieutenants had lost their lives. Among them, on 2 April, was David Carnegie, aged 20. His gentle face, towards the end of his time at school sporting the school prefects' privilege of what was then a fashionable moustache, appears in a number of photographs. He played hockey and rugby, was a school prefect and captain of his house and had a place at King's College, Cambridge, although the war prevented him from ever going into residence. Instead it was to Woolwich, on the strength of Howson's recommendation, that he went, gaining his commission in the RFA in May 1916. He left for the Front almost at once, his battery being in action through the Somme Offensive. Carnegie survived that carnage only to die at the occupation of Elverdinghe Château, near Ypres, the following spring. His colonel wrote warmly, and perhaps predictably, of him as:

> "...a splendidly gallant fellow... He could always be absolutely depended upon and his powers of observation and intuition were exceptional. Everyone, both officers and men were most awfully fond of him."

"One who knew him well" from his schooldays, however, wrote thoughtfully and apparently more conditionally of him:

> "Those who watched David Carnegie at school may have wondered at the measure of his achievement in the different branches of its life. He never appeared to exert himself, yet he became a School Prefect, Captain of his House, a 'first class swimmer', and a valued member of various school teams. How was this done by one who had no exceptional gifts and who neither sought nor desired distinction for himself? It seems somewhat paradoxical until one gives full value to his personality, his determined following of his own line, marked by a true instinct. His apparent diffidence is then seen to be simple modesty, and his success due to well-balanced qualities directed by a resolute will."

Alleyne Boxall and David Carnegie had been friends at school and had last met in January 1917 when they had gone to a play together the day before Carnegie had returned to France for the last time. Boxall had written to David Carnegie's family to express his sympathy on their son's death, as Mrs Carnegie's black-edged reply survives. It is a prime example of the British "stiff upper lip", suspiciously terse and determinedly patriotic. It also includes a reference to the palliative "instantaneous death by shellfire", here vindicated as a comfort to the Hon Mrs Carnegie:

> "David did not suffer, he and the major of his battery were both killed instantaneously by the same shell. I hope you will come safely through. You are an honour and a glory to your country you boys."

Leslie Wills' family, like that of the Hill brothers and Alan Dane, came from Northwood. He was the younger of two brothers at Gresham's and had a particularly hard war. In August 1914 he had joined the Middlesex Regiment with two of his former schoolmasters and several other OGs, but determining to take up the army as a career, he went to Sandhurst. A year later he was serving with the Worcestershire Regiment in Gallipoli. After only four days at the Front he was very seriously wounded in the right lung and sent home immediately. It was not until March 1917 that he was well enough to be sent to France, and even when there he was held at base for two or three weeks. On 18 April he was at last allowed to go to the Front where he was killed by a shell "whilst leading his company into action." Thus the active service at the Front of this keen young soldier totalled precisely nine days. The lieutenant-colonel commanding his battalion scarcely knew him, of course. The most personal tribute came from his commanding officer at the regiment's depot in Cornwall:

> "I have lost a real friend. I tried so hard to keep him here for a further period, as I felt he was not quite fit for the hard campaigning, but he would not let me push it."

A note in the school magazine, unusually, was added to the tributes, probably by Leslie Wills' former housemaster in Woodlands, J. R. Eccles. He commented on Wills' acting talent in school and house plays, and recalled his artistic ability, particularly as a caricaturist. All that was lost in northern France, and Leslie Wills reduced to a name on the Arras Memorial.

The following month, Raymond Berridge was killed in an aeroplane accident, only two days after arriving at his station at Flez, west of St Quentin, near the

Somme. He joined the same squadron, number 6, as Frederick Walker had been in. By 1917 the war fought in the air was very dangerous, more so than fighting on land, not because of fierce dogfights so much as the condition of the aircraft themselves and the inexperience of the pilots. The losses of aircrew by the RFC in the spring and summer of that year became notorious. Berridge's story is very well documented, both by himself and others, and the details are particularly poignant. Winchester Berridge, Raymond's father, took over the entire winding up of the "business" of his son's life, and his family kept letters, photographs and telegrams which tell some of the story of that life from Ray's schooldays to the setting up of the memorials to commemorate the sacrifice of it. A few months before his death, he had written to *The Gresham* recounting the events of his training and his growing number of flying hours. Today that number seems pathetically, suicidally, few, yet in the conditions of early 1917 such a situation was entirely normal:

Raymond Berridge in the uniform of an RNAS officer, 1917.

> "I have had quite a lot of flying, seven hours total in the air and two and a half hours solo. It is a grand sensation and I enjoy it thoroughly. I can manage quite reasonably alone now, and climbed above the clouds to 3,500 feet the other day. ...I have succeeded in making five solo landings without bending an axle even, but you cannot imagine what a pleasant feeling it is to find the machine at rest on terra firma once more after a flight. I can never feel sure that I shall not crash her on landing, as they fly at 60 knots (69 mph) so there is not much time to look about."

He arrived at his station on the afternoon of 1 May, making immediately a very favourable impression on his squadron commander:

> "I could see his worth at a glance. He was so very different in a thousand ways to the average pilot one is given."

That evening this idealistic and conscientious 19-year-old carefully mugged up the maps of the area in preparation for a flight with the squadron the following day:

> "He was tremendously keen. That same evening he made a flight locally, to try the machine; he made a perfect landing. On the 2nd he made two more practice flights, and on the 3rd three more – trying his gun, diving at a target and generally getting used to the machine. He was an exceptionally skilful pilot.

The aeroplane subsequently crashed by Berridge in May 1917.

At 6.0 that evening I took him out with me on an offensive patrol over enemy country. After some time, about 7.0, I noticed that he was missing and had lost touch with us. I returned to the Aerodrome at 8.20 and heard that he had landed at an RFC Aerodrome to find his whereabouts, and, when getting away again to come home, had crashed and been killed. We were tremendously cut up about it, every one of us."

Enquiries revealed that Berridge had landed his Nieuport 17 Bis, a single-seater scout, at the aerodrome of 52 Squadron RFC which was a few miles away at Longavesnes, taken directions and restarted his journey, but the plane had climbed to only 150 feet when:

"…the engine failed. He tried to turn back to the Aerodrome, but in doing so lost speed and the machine spun and fell out of control, hitting the ground with tremendous force, squarely nose on. Death must have been instantaneous.

I have lost the most promising officer I have ever had, and we have all lost a brother officer, who, in only two days had made us love him."

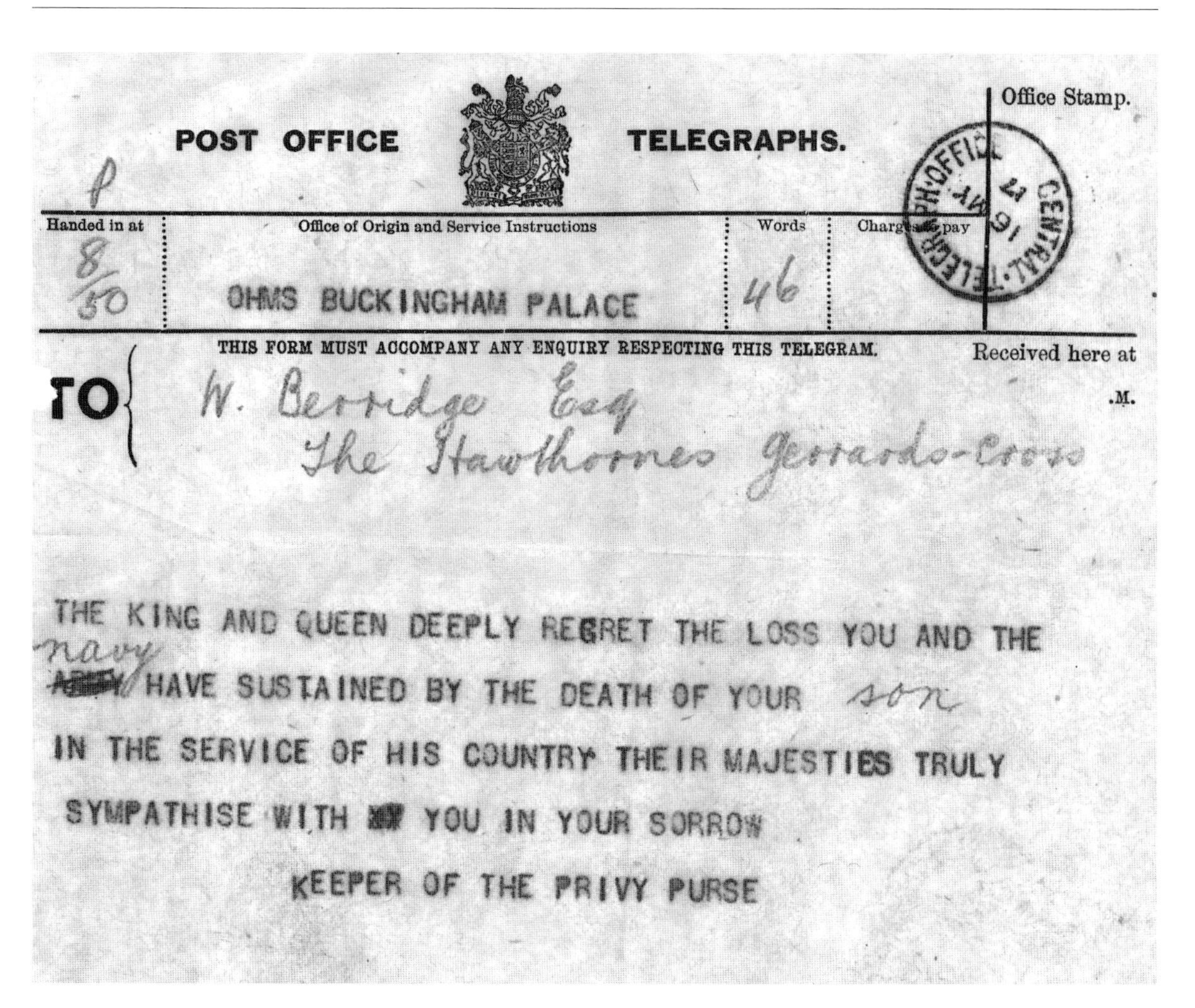

POST OFFICE TELEGRAPHS.

Office Stamp.

p

Handed in at	Office of Origin and Service Instructions	Words	Charges to pay
8/50	OHMS BUCKINGHAM PALACE	46	

THIS FORM MUST ACCOMPANY ANY ENQUIRY RESPECTING THIS TELEGRAM.

Received here at .M.

TO W. Berridge Esq
The Hawthornes Gerrards-Cross

THE KING AND QUEEN DEEPLY REGRET THE LOSS YOU AND THE
~~ARMY~~ navy HAVE SUSTAINED BY THE DEATH OF YOUR son
IN THE SERVICE OF HIS COUNTRY THEIR MAJESTIES TRULY
SYMPATHISE WITH ~~MY~~ YOU IN YOUR SORROW
KEEPER OF THE PRIVY PURSE

The telegram sent to Berridge's parents after his death expressing the sorrow of Their Majesties.

The style of Berridge's CO may seem exaggerated, over-written, but it is echoed by another letter, from the colonel who commanded his battalion when Berridge, as an OTC sergeant, was training signallers for three months in 1915:

> "I am grieved to notice in 'The Times' today the death of your son, who I feel sure must be that splendid boy who was with me at Wycombe, who trained my Signallers and shewed such marked ability. I have never met a young fellow who impressed me more. How proud you must have been of him. England wanted more men like him, but this awful War is taking the best and the bravest."

The telegram sent to his parents is preserved, outrageous by today's standards in its perfunctory message. It was of the form "Delete as appropriate" and read:

> "The King and Queen deeply regret the loss you and the army [*deleted*] navy [*hand-written above*] have sustained by the death of your son [*inserted, hand-written*] in the service of his country Their Majesties truly sympathise with you in your sorrow"

It was "signed" by the Keeper of the Privy Purse. Nevertheless, Raymond's parents kept it.

Howson's letter to Mr and Mrs Berridge, written at a time when he first became seriously ill, has also survived. He wrote:

> "I was greatly shocked to see in today's 'Times' that Raymond has been killed in action. I had heard from him since he went to France, and he sent me a card at Christmas, and he has written to me several times, and I valued his warm-hearted, frank letters, for they reflected his character, and I had a great opinion of his ability – which amounted, I thought nearly to genius. I do not like to think of the depth of sorrow it must be to Mrs Berridge and to you, for Mr Eccles and I know what a gap his death leaves to us – but we can only imagine what it means to you – and our sympathy goes out to you.
>
> His last visit to Holt was a great pleasure to us, and he was full of life and eagerness."

In its lack of careful grammar and phrasing, the letter bespeaks the sincerity of its words.

Raymond Berridge's housemaster in Woodlands, James Eccles, also wrote to the bereaved parents:

> "I recognised your writing this morning with a feeling of dread. I cannot tell you how grieved I am at the news your letter contained. Raymond was in every way a splendid fellow, and I was very proud of him, both for his marked capabilities and his fine character…"

In the collection of his personal effects kept by his father is Berridge's chequebook, the few stubs made out to his military tailor, Gieves, and to the OG Club, the latter in the sum of five shillings. Notes record the return of Raymond's keys, the payment by the Bank of England of 14s 4d, the dividend on War Stock. An advertisement cut from a newspaper enthusiastically endorses the virtues of the "Dayfield Body Shield", bought and ultimately returned from France with

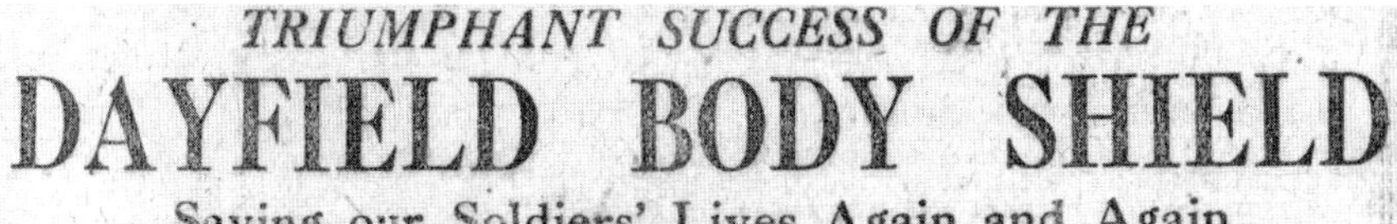

The advertisement for the Dayfield Body Shield on which Berridge's parents had pinned so much hope. The Body Shield they bought was returned with their son's effects in 1917.

Raymond's possessions. A letter from his uncle survives, written all unaware after his nephew's death, the envelope stamped but never addressed, bearing only one word in pencil – "Ray". There is also a letter from Raymond's commanding officer to his father, assuring him in answer to his earlier request that the plane his son was flying was fully airworthy. The desire to find someone or something to blame in such circumstances is sadly understandable, his father struggling to make sense of the apparently senseless.

The letters of condolence flooded in, from Mr Berridge's colleagues, from Myra Hess, the famous pianist, and from Raymond's school friends. One such came from Alec Malcolm, who was to meet his death as an observer in an aeroplane in the following year:

> "Last Wednesday (the 2nd) I met him out here and we talked over things for a bit and he was very bright and happy. Please forgive me for writing, but I thought you'd care to know that he met an old schoolfellow of his a very short time ago who is proud to have known him."

Sebert Humphries, who seems to have taken the deaths of his former school friends particularly hard, wrote touchingly to Mrs Berridge:

> "We said that we would stick together to the end, and we did; but it was not for long. It is the sort of loss that will become greater as time goes on. We had a lovely castle-in-the-air for after the War, when we were each going to take a side-car and a sister round France. We started together in the Old School House. We were together in the Sixth. The week at Gerrards Cross [*Raymond's home*] made us closer. I shall never, never forget our last summer term together; nor his visit to Holt last year and the study tea we had. But best of all was the time when we had a day together at Eastbourne, finishing up with a walk all over Beachy Head in the dark. That was the time when we were closest of all."

In an incident chillingly reminiscent of that which killed Raymond Berridge on 3 May, Adolphe Drey lost his life only days later, on 9 May, the third of six Greshamians who would die in the air that year. Drey, a native of Roubaix in France, had had a hectic war, serving first in France and Gallipoli in 1915. He was present at the evacuation in January 1916, winning an MC for general good services rendered in the field, then went to Egypt as a lieutenant. Towards the end of 1916 he applied for a transfer from the Army Service Corps to the RFC and was clocking up his flying hours in Egypt with 58 Reserve Squadron. His Uncle Oscar received the letter about his death:

> "He had done already about 8 hours flying by himself. He went up in perfect weather early on the morning of the 9th. He had only got up 300 feet when he turned without enough bank and the machine spun and crashed to the ground, breaking into flames. He was unhurt by the fall, but badly burnt and died last night in hospital from shock."

He was stationed at Suez, an important hospital centre during the First World

War, but even prompt treatment could not save him. The account of his death seems illogical, even bizarre. Probably his major was simply trying too hard to console Drey's family.

Two more young Gresham's airmen lost their lives in these months of spring and summer 1917. Captain Donald Cunnell, 5th Hampshire Regiment then RFC, was killed in action on 12 July. His service record has been lost and details of his career through that source are impossible to retrieve. The letter of tribute printed in the school magazine tantalisingly suggested his significant personal contribution, but gave no details:

> "Your son had for months led our formations, and I cannot tell you how much his loss is felt by us all. Only a few days before his death he led a small formation of ours and successfully engaged a very large hostile formation with wonderful results."

An FE2d of the type flown by Donald Cunnell, Gresham's "air ace". As shown in the photograph it looks particularly fragile.

The story behind those few words is fascinating indeed. Donald Cunnell is in fact listed among the air aces of the First World War. He claimed his first hit in May 1917, flying his FE2d with 20 Squadron, and recorded three more victims before July. Then, in the incident alluded to by his colleague, he shot down four German planes on 6 July. That morning Cunnell was taking part in an offensive patrol over Wervicq when he and his fellow pilots, nine of them, encountered a number of German planes, perhaps as many as 40. The British machines formed a circle and tried to make for their own lines, while at the same time attacking the enemy. Donald Cunnell and his observer, Woodbridge, shot down four German planes, and watched another, a red Albatros, spin away apparently out of control. They rightly did not enter a claim as they did not see it crash. It is overwhelmingly likely that the pilot of the Albatros was Manfred von Richthofen, the "Red Baron." It seems that he hit his head and his plane went spinning towards the ground, but at 500ft he came to and managed to land, after which his injuries kept him out of action for a month.

Five days later, the very day before he died, Cunnell claimed another hit, bringing his tally to nine. But in the relentless intensity of the air offensive, in which aircrew faced death every time they climbed into their planes, Donald Cunnell was finally defeated. On 12 July, a day which saw the heaviest air fighting of any in the war thus far, Cunnell was killed by anti-aircraft fire as he was returning from a line patrol over Menin. His courageous observer, Lieutenant Bill, managed to land the plane, but the machine was wrecked and Bill severely shaken.

Alan Jarvis was killed only a month later, on 10 August. He had written to school graphically of his time in the Dardanelles where had taken part both in the landing at Suvla Bay and the evacuation, and had gone from there to Egypt where he was for a time attached to the exotically-named Imperial Camel Corps. He had transferred subsequently to the RFC as an observer, becoming a captain in June 1916. In 1917 he got his wings and joined 1 Squadron at Fienvillers. About three weeks after arriving in France he was killed in a dogfight ten miles over German lines. As Britain was conducting an air offensive, it was not uncommon for aviators to be killed over German-held territory. In this case, the Germans must have buried his body, as he was reburied in Harlebeke New British Cemetery after the Armistice, and lies there today.

Behind the front line of trenches, for some the months of summer had their brighter moments. Alleyne Boxall, stationed near Bethune, wrote of having his photograph taken (12 francs for half a dozen copies) and of "quite a good dinner" the night before:

> "Soup – sardines – Lemon Sole – Chicken salad and new potatoes – chocolate cream – cheese – dessert and coffee. With a bottle of champagne. Beating a rather hasty retreat at the end... such is war!!!"

About a month later, in June, Boxall wrote:

> "I have been in to town to dinner these last two nights with various people so have been rather gay... there was a football match and tomorrow we are arranging some company sports, wheelbarrow, threelegged, sack and obstacle races etc..."

Of course, most of these letters were written during rest periods, and taken out of context may give a misleading impression. It is also true to say that all Alleyne's letters mention war news, some record the death of friends, and others the dangers he himself has encountered, these last brushed off as exciting incidents. Life was not without its happy times, even in France in 1917, but the contrasts could be extreme. A letter written on 2 July speaks of eating cherries and strawberries from the garden; of a dinner with friends in town; of a cycle ride in the summer breeze. Two days later, back in the trenches, Boxall wrote:

> "Last night I had a nasty dose of gas from shells, but am feeling a little better now – so I am taking it easy today. We are living a grand life now – I had breakfast in bed this morning at 10am in the trenches, and intend to continue doing so for the next week or so. Sgt. Davis my platoon sergeant was killed the other night..."

On 16 August, John Beck fell in action. At the age of 28 he was one of the older of the Greshamians and was married with a son. He had come to the school at the same time as Howson, in September 1900, and was one of only seven boarders who were in School House before the school moved to its new site. A Norfolk man, a nephew of Frank Beck who led the Sandringham Company to its mysterious end at Gallipoli, John was commissioned in the Norfolk Regiment in 1915 and went to the Front in August 1916. Later he was transferred to the KRRC, gazetted captain and Adjutant in March 1917. In October of the previous year he had won the MC as a second-lieutenant:

> "He led a party of men against an enemy strong-point with great courage. The attack was completely successful, his party killing one officer and 20 men and taking four prisoners."

His last letter to school was published in *The Gresham* of 31 March 1917.

> "The last two nights too I have been doing a patrol, the second following the result of my first report, as I located a listening post and said so on my report, with the result that last night the General sent up to say I was to take out a fighting patrol of 12 men and try to capture them. Quite all right on paper but it's a little difficult to move 12 men about when you are only 20 yards from Fritz, and he is standing to, being very nervous. The first night I had only just got out through our wire alone when they started bombing and opened fire, so I thought I had been spotted and came in to find out later that the patrol of ours on the right (an officer and a sergeant) had worked into Fritz's trench by mistake. The sergeant was taken prisoner and the officer had an awfully near go, having to be in their wire for half an hour. He came in two hours later badly shaken. Last night my patrol was a wash-out as I had only just got clear of our wire when one of my party slipped into a shell-hole covered with cat's ice – result – much wind on Fritz's part, and many lights, and some firing, so I sent the men back and crawled along to find the post empty – the men must have got in on hearing us. I got very wet and tore my clothes pretty well, but did not get up until three this afternoon so feel much refreshed now."

Days before his death, John Beck was recommended for second-in-command of a battalion, a post he never, of course, took up. The Becks have an account which has come down through their family about the notification of John Beck's death. John had five brothers, one of whom, Victor, was also at Gresham's, and who survived the war. Two others were killed, Alec with his Uncle Frank at Suvla Bay, and Evelyn at Gaza. One day John's wife received the Army telegram she dreaded. When she opened it she found that it referred to the death, not of her husband, but of his brother, Captain E. Beck. With deeply mixed feelings of sorrow and relief she took the telegram to her sister-in-law. As she handed it over she was given in its place another telegram, also wrongly addressed, which contained the news of John's death. The shock to both the women must have been appalling, the double blow to the parents of the brothers shattering.

The tribute to John Beck from his colonel gives details of the circumstances of the death of a man in this case well known to the writer:

> "I never knew anyone so unobtrusively and persistently brave. His sympathy and care for his men was so deeply genuine that he had no time to worry about his own danger. A message came that a man had been wounded lightly just outside his dugout. He dashed out with the brandy flask, and having given the man a drink, was talking to him when a shell burst fairly near and a small piece hit his chest. He went unconscious at once and died from haemorrhage. It was a bad moment for all of us, for he was loved by everyone. Even to me out here, who am in constant contact with death, it was the greatest shock, for we all valued and loved him. I have never known anyone more genuinely and deeply mourned."

For once, cheerfulness seems to have been a genuine characteristic of the man, mentioned in all three letters written to his family by fellow officers after his death.

Robert Inglis' wartime career was desperately short. He volunteered for the RFC in March 1917, when aged only 17 years and seven months, and arrived in France on 9 September, a pilot with 19 Squadron. Sent up to the lines on 19th, he was shot down with two other machines from his squadron on the 21st:

> "Your son was sent out with five other aeroplanes at about nine o'clock yesterday morning. They had crossed the line when they were suddenly attacked from above by an unusual number of enemy machines. A general fight ensued in which one of the enemy machines was destroyed but afterwards only three of our six machines came back."

The story is plain enough. Inglis died in German-held territory and was buried by the Germans. The first news to his parents held out some hope, the telegram pointing out that their boy was "Missing, not necessarily wounded or killed". Almost a month later their hopes were dashed when they were told that the Germans had found his Spad one-seater, with the "occupant dead". The German government returned his effects – his cheque book, two cigarette cases, one leather, one silver, his prayer book and a rosary. More extraordinary was the wealth of this very young man. At a time when the estate of most Greshamians was less than £300, Inglis left the staggering sum of £24,540 3s 6d.

A Trial of Endurance

BY THE middle of 1917 the war was destroying the resilience of men on both sides. By now there was a feeling that this was a conflict of attrition, which could neither be fought with confidence and optimism, nor abandoned for the sake of the thousands who had already lost their lives. Howson seems to have felt pessimistic at this time that the war would end with stalemate. For Gresham's the relentless list of the fallen continued to grow, encompassing some of the most revered of the headmaster's boys.

One such was Neill Newsum. The school records afford many references to him, as he was the captain of Howson's house and school captain from September 1914 to July 1915. He appears on many photographs, gazing solemnly into the camera through wire-rimmed spectacles, and looking to modern eyes perhaps rather older than his years. The fact that he was promoted to the rank of captain in the 5th Battalion Lincolnshire Regiment at the age of 21 also suggests, in another sense, an old head on young shoulders. Newsum had been sent to Ireland in April 1916 at the time of the Easter Rising before he saw service in France from February 1917. He fell near Ypres on 26 September that same year, killed by heavy shellfire after his company had reached its objective. His colonel described "his soldierly qualities and kind disposition" while a comrade wrote:

> "He was a long way the best company commander in the battalion, essentially unselfish, thoughtful for his men, the essence of common sense and thoroughness, with a wonderful pride in his Company, a pride which his men answered to and never betrayed."

Less than two weeks later, Ernest Elwell was killed in the same area, also in the Third Battle of Ypres. He had hoped very much to join the RFC but his eyesight was not good enough and so he became an infantryman. Life in the trenches was even more difficult for him than it was for most as he suffered from severe eczema. This condition was worsened, in the words of his medical report, "by army diet and exposure to the cold and wet". He must have been in acute discomfort, even pain, almost all the time.

At the beginning of October he was serving with the 21st Manchester Regiment, preparing to attack the higher ground south of Polygon Wood and north past Zonnebeke and Poelcappelle. On the evening of 2 October, Elwell and his comrades had to shelter in the filthy dugouts of Zillebeke but by late the following evening they had arrived at Polygon Wood, a position very heavily shelled by the Germans. On the morning of 4 October the attack began, and so did the rain. At first the Allies made good progress, but the German defence held, making the task of the 21st Manchesters very difficult. Elwell was killed by a shell on 6 October, one of four officers in the battalion who fell. Ten others were wounded along with 35 men killed, 148 wounded and 19 missing of the other ranks.

A miniature of Captain Neill Newsum, who died in 1917, one week before his 21st birthday.

About a fortnight later, Raymond Thicknesse, another former head of school, was killed while serving with the Lancashire Fusiliers, also near Ypres, in the fighting of 9 October known as the Battle of Poelcappelle. On his father's death, Raymond had been adopted by his uncle and aunt, and after a splendid school career he went up to Pembroke College, Cambridge, with a Classical Exhibition, returning to study law in his uncle's office. The school record shows him as a good all-rounder, playing school rugby from an early age, breaking school athletics records – for the broad jump, for example – as well as excelling academically. He seems to have cared about his appearance too, growing a moustache once he was a school prefect and posing nonchalantly in several group photographs. According to Richard Holmes, the Battle of Poelcappelle "went wrong from the start". The mud was appalling and the artillery did not manage to destroy the enemy machine-gun emplacements, which remained swathed in lethal barbed wire. Of the manner of Thicknesse's death there is no direct record, save that he died, like so many other second-lieutenants, "whilst gallantly leading his men". Of his personality little more is known, the only sources two short tributes from his colonel and a French officer.

The Colonel described him as:

> "...always most cheery and his jolly smile under the most adverse conditions was always a great help to the men of his platoon. His death is keenly felt by us all."

Not a great deal of store can be placed upon such a clichéd statement at this stage of the war. But the French account is more personal and thoughtful, as well as to English taste perhaps a little florid:

> "Je m'étonnais de trouver sous cette robuste et mâle apparence tant de douceur, tant de sentimentalité. On sentait une immense bonté dans ce coeur et une intelligence, qui sans aimer parader ni éblouir, éclairait de toute sa clarté le sanctuaire intérieur de sa belle âme."
> [*I was surprised to find, behind his solid masculine exterior, such gentleness and sensitivity, I felt that there was great goodness in his heart, goodness which, without drawing attention to itself or dazzling, cast its light on the inner workings of his beautiful soul.*]

It seems that Thicknesse was buried on the battlefield, and it was with many apologies and assurances that the War Office wrote to his family in 1920 to explain the need for his exhumation to the British War Cemetery in Poelcappelle. Thicknesse was one of the few Greshamians who made a will. Despite the fact that he had been adopted by his uncle and aunt, he bequeathed his medals to his mother.

Raymond Thicknesse, school captain in 1909, leading rugby player at school and for Pembroke College, Cambridge, killed at the battle of Poelcappelle, October 1917.

The October 1917 edition of the school magazine published the last letters of Greshamians fighting in the war. The reasons for this are obscure. Howson, of course, had been very ill earlier in the year and if the letters were contributed through him, then it may be that he had simply been too ill to think of such a task. Perhaps the men stopped writing, or started saying things that Howson did not want to publish. Perhaps there was a sense of losing heart in keeping up such a correspondence. Whatever the reason, the letters ceased to appear. There was still the impulse to report on favourable news, however. The cricket team was undefeated as late as the end of July, quite a contrast to the 1914 season. The new shooting range was a great success, as was the Shakespeare Society. Perhaps most noteworthy was that Geoffrey Gwyther, who had almost been compelled to shoot one of his men for insubordination in 1915, had composed four songs which were sung by the school's head of music, Geoffrey Shaw, in a recital in the summer of 1917. This, according to the school magazine, was the first time "we had heard any compositions by an Old Boy. We should like to hear these again – they are worth another hearing." Gwyther had also set to music seven poems from William Blake's *Songs of Innocence*, and was highly complimented by Shaw as a folksongist.

While the school took understandable refuge in English traditional games, drama and music, its former pupils continued to suffer in France. Arthur Cole had gone into banking after he left school and in 1909 had gone out to Canada as an employee of the Bank of Canada in Montreal. He moved to live in a silver mining district 50 miles from the railway, which had to be reached by steamboats on the lakes, finding that he liked life in a mining camp better than life in the city. By the time of the outbreak of war he was living in British Columbia and in 1915 joined the Canadian Mounted Rifles. He came to England in July 1916, then went on to France in August 1917 attached to a battalion of the British Columbia Regiment. The account of his death given in the school magazine has a sinister ring. He was:

> "last seen on the morning of 10 November waiting to 'go over' in the attack on the Passchendaele Ridge and he has never been heard of since."

Passchendaele, just outside the ruined town of Ypres, has become a byword for its wastes of mud and numberless loss of men. Famously, Siegfried Sassoon summed it up in his poem *Memorial Tablet* in the words, "I died in hell – (They called it Passchendaele)." The tanks which it had been hoped would destroy the iron-meshed German pill-boxes simply sank, and it took the Allied soldiers from July to November to reach and take the Passchendaele Ridge, a distance of only about nine kilometres. It is no accident that the largest British war cemetery in the world, Tyne Cot, with its 12,000 graves and memorial to 34,000 missing, is at the top of the ridge.

Another Greshamian, Douglas Brownsword, a captain with the KRRC, died of wounds received at Passchendaele Ridge on Christmas Day 1917. Once again he apparently suffered a single wound, this time to the spine, and died after a few hours. He was the only son of a Nottingham lace maker, who had bought Rollesby Hall near Great Yarmouth, presumably with the profits from a successful business in which his son joined him for a short while. Brownsword went up to

Caius College, Cambridge, to study Natural Science in 1909, and enjoyed a varied sporting career there, playing in the lawn-tennis six for his college as well as in the hockey team, as left-half. He won some praise from the writer of the notes on the "Characters of the Team" who was not afraid to be critical. "A really sound half who played well throughout the season. To be really good should mark his man more closely." Good advice for the sports field no doubt, but of little use at Passchendaele.

Some young men had remarkable escapes before they were finally lost in battle. Geoffrey Frost had tried to get a commission in 1915, but as he met delays he went to serve as a private in the Royal Fusiliers in January 1916. Arriving in France in July of that year, he was wounded for the first time in October and again in September 1917. On that occasion, only he and one other man of his platoon returned to safety. He rejoined his battalion at the end of that month, and was with them when they fought at Cambrai on 30 November. The battle had begun ten days earlier with a massed rank of over 400 tanks to tackle the difficulties of the terrain. After an encouraging beginning for the Allies, the Germans began to set up a stern defence and the tanks began to develop problems. Some 65 had been destroyed but over 110 more had broken down or been abandoned. Because the troops were so weary their commanders had been ordered to rest, their seconds-in-command thus being in charge when the German counter-offensive began on the 30th. Frost was lost in the ferocity of battle, never seen or heard of again among the 40,000 allied casualties.

By December 1917 the editor of *The Gresham*, along with many other Britons, was taking a gloomy view of recent developments:

> "The hand of internal discord has laid hold of unhappy Russia; not only is she weakened seriously, but there is a lurking chance that she may withdraw from the Alliance... We have heard some people assert that in a case of dire need the German people could always hold out longer than our own people, by virtue of their great system of bureaucratic discipline. We, as a nation, must show that free will is better than the forces of terror."

The editor was right to highlight the dangers of Russia's withdrawal after her own revolution, because for the first time in the war the German forces did not have to fight on two fronts. All their energies could be turned to a spring offensive in France, and for Gresham's, as for the nation at large, this led to the greatest number of casualties of any of the war years. There were to be 31 more OGs killed by the end of the war. The school magazine reflected the crisis by reducing most of its reports to the most perfunctory review. Lectures, debates and society meeting were listed, but there was no descriptive detail. The editor, it seems, was either lazy or disheartened. Only one item in the edition of December 1917 raised the tone above the mundane and war-obsessed, the acquisition by the school library of a document of 1547 on vellum, bearing the signature of Sir John Gresham, and to be displayed thereafter in the gallery of Big School. Otherwise the finer points of the chapel potato patch and a numbing account of the Gresham's School War Savings Association were the issues given most column inches. Depressingly, and in marked contrast to most items in the magazine, the list of Greshamians serving in the war by now stretched to nine pages.

The first OG death of 1918 was in unusual circumstances. Cedric Fox had transferred from the Royal Fusiliers to the RNAS and had taken part in several anti-Zeppelin patrols in the United Kingdom during August 1916 before being sent to Italy. He was reported "missing, feared drowned" off the coast of southern Italy on Monday, 7 January. Having asked to go in pursuit of an enemy submarine sighted near a patrol boat, at 2pm he left his station at Otranto with his observer, Jones. It is certain that they were still airborne over the Adriatic at 3.10pm when they sent a message, because their seaplane had to be in flight in order to send a wireless signal, but at 3.45pm they liberated a pigeon with a note saying they were on the sea eight miles SSW of Saseno. Much responsibility rested on this innocent creature. At this point a storm intervened with fatal consequences. The pigeon lost its way in the bad weather, and did not arrive back at the station until the following morning. The boats went immediately to search, but found only the wreckage of the seaplane, with no sign of its crew. The official report said only: "There was a very heavy sea running that afternoon and a gale got up, so that everything was against them."

By the second decade of the 20th century, Howson had transformed Gresham's from a predominantly local grammar school into a nationally-known public boarding school, but there were, of course, a number of local boys who attended as day pupils. Three such were to die in the early weeks of 1918. Far away from the Western Front and far away from his home in Paston, North Norfolk, Harold Cobon died of wounds sustained at the siege of Jerusalem. After school he had farmed near his home, and in 1911 had joined the Norfolk Yeomanry. Thus he was called up on the first day of the war, already a lance-corporal. Promoted to the rank of corporal in November 1914, he was a sergeant by April 1915, and in September went out to Gallipoli. He took his commission in April 1916, and in November returned to Egypt with his old regiment, taking part in the Palestine Campaign. It was in the Battle of Shiria that he won his Military Cross:

> "...for conspicuous gallantry and devotion to duty. He showed great initiative and judgement in a difficult situation and set a splendid example to his men by his courage and contempt of danger under heavy fire."

However, Cobon was wounded at the siege of Jerusalem in December 1917 and the following month died of those wounds. He is buried in the Cairo War Memorial Cemetery. After his death his colonel, who had recommended him for the MC, wrote a letter to Cobon's parents to whom their son's medal was posthumously presented, giving a few more details of fighting in the Middle East:

> "His Company was lying out in the open, holding the ground already won, for several hours, being heavily shelled by the Turks. During all this time your son and his Company Commander saved their Company from heavy casualties by their coolness and contempt of danger, and by showing their initiative in moving their men from place to place. I cannot say anything too high in praise of your son, both as a soldier and as a man... During the battles of Shiria and Beersheba he was first-rate, as I can tell from personal experience as I was in command of the regiment then, and there was never a Military Cross better earned than the one he got. He did splendidly also, I hear, in the battle in which he was wounded. His death is a very heavy blow to the regiment and both officers and men will feel the loss very deeply."

Two more local old boys of Gresham's, almost the same age, Frederick Chestney and Henry Beeton, died within two days of one another in early 1918, and were buried in Norfolk only a few miles apart: Chestney in Holt and Beeton in Weybourne. The school list for Midsummer 1912 shows them together in Lower Remove. Chestney had worked as a student teacher at Holt Council School from 1915. Having attested before he was 18, he was called up in March 1917, just a month after his 18th birthday. He was later given the rank of lance-corporal and appointed a teacher in an army school. From May 1917, however, he became seriously ill and was in hospital until July when he was discharged from the army. On 30 January 1918 he died of phthisis, now known as tuberculosis, never having seen the active service he was so keen to undertake.

Beeton died in a flying accident near Huntingdon on 1 February 1918. At his funeral were 16 Gresham's OTC members in uniform, some scarcely younger than the man they mourned. His grave, now sadly damaged and overgrown, describes him as the only son of Robert and Julia Beeton and gives his age as 18. It is altogether a sombre sight, shrouded in the shadow of the 13th-century priory at Weybourne, and dark even on a summer's afternoon.

John Wright also fell in February 1918. A surviving photograph of him shows a handsome and serious young man, and his Junior School portrait reveals a child determined and solemn even at the age of about 12. In 1915 he had seen service with the Horse Artillery in Egypt, but in 1916 went to the Front with the RFA. He had advanced with the Royal Field Artillery in the latter part of 1917 to the neighbourhood of Boezinge near Ypres, which for most of the war directly faced the German front line, and was killed "instantaneously" on 24 February 1918 whilst doing duty as a liaison officer. Buried initially in the fields outside the village, his grave was moved only after the Armistice.

The Black Crisis

THE spring of 1918 found the editor of *The Gresham* in irritated mood. Criticism of the continuing conduct of the war was clearly to the fore, and he used his column to deplore this in terms reminiscent of an impatient nanny:

> "We live in the midst of destructive criticism, wherever we go, but very few of those who employ it have any right to do so. Most of us display a complete lack of the scientific mind. We are continually tempted to take a superficial view of things and not to realise the many difficulties lying underneath the surface. The nation is not in need of critics; it is unfortunately too much hampered by them already. If we do not agree with what others have done in the past we must prepare ourselves to do better in the future."

By April, the editor was no more cheerful, was indeed if anything more bitter. To many at school the war meant nothing, he asserted"

> "...beyond a matter for occasional interest. It is indeed hard to realise that just across the sea is modern warfare in all its ugliness, where men are suffering death and injury so that we may enjoy the calm beauty of an English spring in peace... We are living in a little world of our own, where there is no war. There is nothing to suggest that the whole country is employed in its preparations for the killing of men, unless perhaps it be the newspapers, with their convenient headlines for those who condescend to contemplate the present crisis."

Some of the boys felt this kind of attack was a little unfair. Geoffrey Diggle agreed that there was seldom talk of the war among the boys, but pointed out that it was far from easy to find out war news as the only newspaper in his house was one copy of *The Times* among 30 boys, left in the dining hall after the housemaster had finished reading it. As the boys were not allowed to sit in the dining hall between meals, the headlines had to be glimpsed while standing up. This fact did not stop their housemaster, the Reverend F. G. E. Field, from haranguing them:

> "While you in your selfishness spend your time pulling the damper out and nearly blowing the boiler up to get hotter water for your wretched baths, our men at the Front advance ten miles through thick mud. But how many of you either know this or care? What does it matter to you compared with a spoonful of jam?"

The editor of the magazine was right to speak of a crisis, however, as the Germans launched their Spring Offensive on 21 March. In the following eight days, unknown by early April to those at school in Holt, six Greshamians died in France.

Denys Rogers died only hours into the Spring Offensive on 21 March. He was serving as a second-lieutenant with the RFA and was at his post with the guns when he was killed by the explosion of a shell during the five-hour preliminary bombardment preceding the German advance on that first morning. He was at first hit on the arm, and taken to the nearest gun pit for shelter, when it was destroyed by a shell which killed him and two other men. Rogers had had interesting plans for his life after the war. Having already spent time in Spain to learn the language, he intended to settle in South America. Returning from Spain, by this time old enough to gain a commission, although still only 18½, he joined the RFA. His experience exemplified the statistics of life expectancy on the Western Front. When he was killed, he had been there for precisely two weeks. His body could not be extricated from the wreckage of the gun pit as the army, being outflanked, had to retire, leaving the remains of the three soldiers in enemy territory. Thus, he is remembered on the Arras Memorial.

By the time the words of the April editorial were written, the most decorated OG to lose his life in the war, Adrian Graves, had been killed in battle, but the news had not yet reached school. The younger brother of Cecil Graves, who was sitting out the war in German captivity, he was also one of the young men mourned by his former teacher Dallas Wynne Willson as one of the brightest boys he had ever taught. His was a glittering school career indeed. He was a school prefect and won an Exhibition to Balliol College, Oxford, at the age of 17, but was there for only two months before he obtained his commission in his local regiment, the Norfolks. From there he transferred to the Machine Gun Corps in which he served continuously in France for 18 months, winning decorations at both the Somme and at Messines Ridge. On the Somme he gained his MC for his work near Bailiff Wood on 10 July:

> "...Under heavy fire he brought his guns into action to repel a sudden attack at close quarters. On many occasions he has shown great bravery in attack."

PRAYER FOR STEADFASTNESS.

Dear Master, Grant that each day I may accept cheerfully the work thou givest me to do. Help me to do it earnestly and with steadfastness, not judging it according to inclination or aversion, but according to thy will. The path thou hast bidden me to tread is the path of salvation, and by walking in it with a right spirit it is my inestimable privilege to help Thee. Let this thought be ever in my heart. May I learn to 'look beyond results' and by constantly striving after forgetfulness of self, rise up every day more firmly resolved to fight thy battles. And may I do all to the Greater Glory of God. Amen.

A copy of the daily prayer "For Steadfastness" found on the body of Adrian Graves, MC and Bar.

At Messines Ridge he won his Bar to the MC for:

> "...Conspicuous gallantry and initiative. During an attack by his Brigade he encountered very heavy fire on his way to the objective, and on reaching it found the place untenable. After having three men killed, and although himself wounded in the head and hand, he moved his guns forward to our front line and remained in action for 48 hours, superintending his guns without relief and with great ability. Throughout the operations he showed a fine example of endurance and cheerfulness."

Adrian Graves wrote to school from France, and one of his letters, only a paragraph or two away from the official citation in *The Gresham*, describes the scene at Messines Ridge, near Hill 60, from his point of view. His modest and understated account makes a revealing contrast:

> "Three times in two hours I had the most extraordinarily narrow escapes. Each time I was hit, on the hand, on the side of the head, and the foot, but I was only scratched. In one case I was standing at the entrance to a dugout. The dugout was blown in by a shell, two men in it were killed, and I was covered in earth. I found two holes in my putties and had a sore ankle for a couple of days. We were most extraordinarily lucky, I was the only officer touched, and we had no NCOs wounded. Three of my men were killed in the dugout and three more were wounded."

Only two days before his death Graves was promoted to the rank of captain, dying as he had lived, with great bravery, on 22 March 1918. The entry in the Balliol College Register gives some details of the events surrounding his death:

> "On March 22nd he was in command of the machine-gunners who, after two hours heavy shelling from 6am held Henin Hill till 3pm against what seemed overwhelming masses of the enemy, and only then fell back, when ordered, with their guns. Wounded in the thigh, he carried on, but was wounded again and disabled. He was being carried off by his Sergeant-Major when he was killed instantaneously by a bullet in the head. It was a remarkable career for one who seemed marked out to be a student and a writer."

The tributes to him were particularly heartfelt, the accounts revealing the fierceness of the fighting, the courage of the soldiers and the ultimate futility of the lives lost in "preventing the enemy from taking the hill for a whole day." The remark was, of course, made with pride, but seems a small triumph indeed set against the loss of "a very, very Christian gentleman", and one who "placed his duty before his interest to so great an extent." It is naive to judge by appearances, but certainly his gentle scholarly face and thoughtful demeanour on the school photographs which survive do not suggest the archetypal man of action. He carried with him a copy of his daily prayer, "For Steadfastness" which was found with him when he was killed.

His uncle, Lord Edward Grey of Falloden, who was very fond of his nephews, wrote on 28 March to Adrian's brother Cecil, still interned in Holland:

> "It is very bitter and sad for you that Adrian is gone and you won't see him. I feel it very much, for the fine character that the war brought out in him and his attractive nature and cleverness made us all love and admire him…But it is of your mother that we have to think now. I do not feel that we ought to be sorry for Adrian: if the object of life is to live without reproach, to become a fine character and to act nobly, then Adrian's life has been a complete success."

The school tribute to him was once again of the "special" type.

> A.H.G.
> School Prefect, 1914
> A life of great promise – a radiant spirit.
> In School and House he was a strong rock, and among OGs a pillar – where pillars are many.
> With eyes fixed longingly on Oxford and the subsequent "making of men" as a Master, fighting was to him but a duty to be faithfully done, in spite of its ugliness, its pitiful destruction.
> Greatly gifted, he was further endowed with a wonderful charm that came from the heart.
> His devotion to his School was surpassed only by his love of Home.
> The gap he leaves seems irreparable.

Howson seems to have thought that Adrian Graves would teach, his Oxford colleagues that he would write, but both sources comment on the dissonance between his interests and his military career. His photograph in uniform is enigmatic, but perhaps bears out the assessment of him given in the College Register:

> "He… altogether gave much promise for the future, borne out by a certain quiet firmness of character and an even temper which meant self-control and no undue placidity."

The worst day of the war in terms of Greshamian deaths was 22 March 1918. On that day fell not only Adrian Graves, but two others as well. George Hawksley died in No 38 Casualty Clearing Station, from multiple gunshot wounds received in the retreat in the Somme area. His excellent letters home, detailed and informative as well as powerful and deeply felt, have been quoted earlier. As ever, hardship was belittled, no matter what the internal turmoil. "I was mud nearly to the waist, but felt pretty comfortable", and "it was a very trying business altogether," were astounding understatements in the context of the letters' descriptions. A letter from a fellow officer sent to Hawksley's young widow, who had been a wife for less than three years, reveals what little more we know of the man:

> "He was one of the great friends I made in France. He was the life and soul of our mess; everyone was so fond of him, the men as well as the officers. He never seemed to be put out over anything, or ever said an unkind word of anyone. I am sure that, even at such a terrible time, you will be proud to learn that his regiment has been the sole topic of talk here! They simply covered themselves with glory. Although attacked time after time by superior numbers, they did not give a foot of ground."

What began as a depressingly familiar encomium became an individual appreciation of the part played by Hawksley and his fellows. On 22 March, Captain Henry Chapman MC also met his death, leading some infantry in a counter attack. An excellent horseman, he passed out tenth from Woolwich in 1913 and received his commission in the Royal Artillery. As a career soldier he went to France immediately on the outbreak of war and was one of the first in the Expeditionary Force to come into close contact with the enemy, at Mons.

As he reached his position he heard digging in front which he had been told was fellow soldiers "digging in". Some of his men began to sing. The digging stopped. Rifles were fired, and he and his men beat a very hasty retreat.

Wounded on 8 September at the Battle of the Marne, Chapman was invalided home for two months, but after November 1914 he did not leave France and Belgium except to take a battery commander's course which he passed with 100 per cent marks and, naturally, the first position in the group. He was again mentioned in despatches and awarded the MC in January 1917. By the time of the German Offensive of March 1918 he was commanding "G" Battery of the RHA and was seen to fall on the 22nd. He was carried, wounded, to a dugout by the enemy, after which he was never seen again. A brief report in *The Gresham* noted that Chapman, O. S. D. Wills and J. C. Ellis were missing, Wills not returning after being sent out on patrol to gain information. The stories of Osborne Wills, the elder brother of Leslie, and Clive Ellis unfolded later, but there was never any further account of Chapman's death and so it was one year later, on the grounds of the "lapse of time", that the Army Council agreed that he was dead. His finest tribute was also the shortest. A staff officer said in a letter to Chapman's father:

"I loved your boy so much; he was so full of spirits and so brave."

Another Gresham's MC was killed in action on Sunday, 24 March 1918 on the Somme, near Albert. The Fifth Army, "Kitchener's Army", was being driven back by overwhelming numbers across the old battlefields of the Somme, and both William Barker and his younger brother Harold were involved in that retreat. William was a solicitor by profession, but he was also the son of a colonel and had enlisted in August 1914 as a trooper in the 15th Hussars. By December he had gained his commission in the DLI and remained with that regiment until his death, by which time he had risen to the rank of captain. At the Battle of Loos, in September 1915, an action notable for the atrocious losses suffered by the British Army – 8,000 killed in one hour – he was recommended for his calmness and gallantry in leading his platoon.

While acting as battalion bombing officer, Barker was wounded by being shot through the left thigh at Fricourt on 1 July 1916, the first day of the Somme. This happened at 9am and he lay on the field all day, still directing his men, until he was picked up at 8.30pm the following day. Not surprisingly he was incapacitated for six months after that but he was awarded his MC on 1 January 1917 in recognition of his courage, as well as being given a captaincy. Later that year, in May, at about the same time as William returned to France, his younger brother Arnold succumbed to the effects of the gas attack two years previously. Now, in the week beginning 24 March 1918, two more brothers were to die. A fellow officer of William Barker wrote to Colonel Barker describing his eldest son's death.

> "This is the most difficult letter I have ever written and in it I want to tell you how Old Billy was killed. The Battalion, as you will know, was involved in the withdrawal from 21 March until 2 April. During the first few days your son's Company ('C') and mine ('D') constantly supported and helped each other out of exceedingly difficult situations. We were together always, our Company Headquarters were together and we advised each other on all things. All went well until the 24th when your son was given a most critical flank to hold, in front of Clery-sur-Somme. We had hard hand-to-hand fights with the enemy, and, though in vastly superior numbers and with vastly superior effectives, 'C' Coy. beat him off and held him off until the fight had gone on for 2 and a half hours. Then, after a perfect shoal of cylindrical stick bombs, he drove us back by sheer weight of numbers. Billie and one of his officers were killed instantaneously by one of the bombs. It is almost

Two of the Barker brothers from Sunderland. On the left is William (MC) and on the right Harold. They died within five days of each other in March 1918. The family had lost another son, Arnold, from the effects of gas poisoning the previous year.

> unnecessary for me to tell you how he was loved and admired by everyone; you know that it has always been so. He has left a big gap out here, a gap which I feel more than anyone else."

Harold Barker followed in his elder brother's footsteps in various ways. He too had a distinguished career at school – as school prefect and captain of his house he was almost as eminent as William, who was head of school in 1904, and he too qualified as a solicitor in his father's office. He joined a Durham regiment, the Durham Garrison Artillery, but transferred to the RFA and went to France with the Wearside Brigade in 1915. He was mentioned in despatches in the New Year's Honours List of 1917 and shortly before his death was promoted to the rank of major. He was killed on Good Friday, 29 March 1918 by the explosion of a shell on the forward observation post while on duty there. The letter sent to his wife gives more details.

> "On the 28th he did magnificent work. The Bosche attacked us heavily then; he was full of zeal and keenness, and did several very

> dangerous messages for me, when I had no one else to send. That evening I asked him to go to a forward observation post, which we had to man, as I had only one other officer left fit for duty. He was killed there the following morning."

A fellow officer, a subaltern, also wrote to Mrs Barker.

> "The day before, during the battle he was simply splendid, an example of cheerfulness and courage that inspired the whole battery...he himself volunteered to take it in turns with the subalterns up at the O.P. He relieved me there the night before he was killed. He was as cheery as anything at the time, and one has the consolation of knowing he was killed instantaneously."

It is difficult to imagine the effect that the deaths of two such fine young men would have on their family, particularly after the loss of their son Arnold the year before. At school the magazine recorded the deaths in an emphatic way.

> C.W.T.B.
> Captain of School 1904.
> H.F.B.
> School Prefect 1908.
> Par nobile fratrum! Deeply attached in life – in death not divided.
> In different ways, without a thought of claiming it, they won the love of those who knew them best. They deservedly were held in high esteem by all.
> In the one there was a conscience so clear, so clean, that the only fear to us was of his unnecessary self-depreciation.
> In the other a cheerfulness growing out of an abiding sense of right.
> In both, wonderful courage, unswerving loyalty and a great good comradeship. Friends to have and to hold and to be thankful for.

It is not clear who wrote these "special" obituaries, but it is sure that no one was in a better position to do so than Howson himself. William Barker was a founding member of the new school, "one of that first set of boys who helped to lay the foundations of the Present school traditions."

There were, at one time or another, five Barker brothers at Gresham's so we cannot know to which of them Howson was referring when he named a stream in Wharfedale "Barker's Brook", but it is most likely that it was for William.

Considering the happy holidays that Howson spent with the boys, teaching them to fish and enjoy the countryside, and taking into account his ongoing illness, the death of this young man must have been a great blow to the headmaster.

Alongside the names of William and Harold Barker on the Pozières Memorial is that of one other Greshamian, Harry Robinson, who died on 26 March. After school he had gone to Malaya where he was a rubber planter, and before the outbreak of war had joined the Malay Volunteers. When he died he was a captain in the Rifle Brigade, killed "instantaneously", like so many others, and lost without trace.

As the Spring Offensive continued, the young men of Gresham's suffered losses along all the line of the enemy advance. Thomas Sillem, a captain in the Welch Regiment, was killed by a shell at Lindenhoek on 14 April 1918, eight months after he had won his MC:

> "...for conspicuous gallantry and devotion to duty in taking up a battalion pack convoy with rations and ammunition for six consecutive days under very hostile fire and in very bad weather. His organisation of the transport under exceptionally trying circumstances was admirable."

Sillem had joined the Territorial Force as a motorcyclist because he was the proud owner of a Triumph Standard Model 3½hp, bought in 1913 for the sum of £50. By the time of his death he had changed his mode of transport to the four-legged sort – one of his few trivial debts on his death was the wage due to his groom.

Clive Ellis, as a second-lieutenant in the Tank Corps, followed an unusual path amongst Greshamians. He had gone out to France in January 1918, aged at that time only 19. Unusually, too, there is a detailed record of his appearance, given by another English officer:

> "...tall, thin, with a fresh coloured complexion, large dark eyes, black curly hair, prominent cheekbones, aquiline nose."

Ellis was asthmatic, which might have accounted at least in part for his slender physique. His Majesty's Landships, as tanks were officially known, had been introduced in September 1916 but were notoriously unreliable. Only one other Greshamian had been in the Tank Corps, Ernest Mobbs, and he had died of enteric fever in 1916 before he could have realised the potential of these fearsome machines. By the time of the Battle of Cambrai in 1917, they were used in large numbers – 400 in that battle – and were much more of a force. In the retreat of 22 March, Ellis brought his tank out of action, destroyed it, and was then seriously wounded by sniper fire in the left thigh and declared missing. He had been taken prisoner and was in Feld Lazaret 55 (a German field hospital). In 1920 the official report of his final illness and death was sent to his mother by the Berlin Military Mission, who gave details from the doctor who attended Clive Ellis as follows:

> "On account of gas phlegmone [*gas gangrene*] the leg had to be amputated. This officer was a very quiet and a very grateful patient. He died [*on 21 April*] of increasing blood poisoning and was buried in the same manner as the German officers in the beautifully situated cemetery of Villers-Faucon."

Gas gangrene was the cause of death of many soldiers in the First World War, occurring as infection entered wounds left unattended for long periods of time in the aftermath of battles. But this story had a twist. The account of the German doctor continued:

> "In the lazaret an English officer of the name of Osborne Wells (who was wounded slightly in the knee) assisted me in the care of the English wounded, because I cannot speak English. I spoke French with him… I asked Mr Osborne Wells to go and see him once more as he was dying."

Beneath the letter was Osborne "Wells'" address. By an astounding coincidence, the young officer who visited Ellis and tried to comfort him was an Old Greshamian, Osborne Wills, the older brother of Leslie Wills. Neither knew that they had attended the same school, as Wills left as Ellis arrived, but it is strange to think of two OGs brought together in such a place all unknowing, by the chances of war. About 20 April, Wills visited Clive Ellis for the last time.:

> "I… found the officer very weak and relapsing into unconsciousness… (he) could barely recognise me, and after endeavouring to obtain some message from him I had to leave him."

Wills put on record the efforts of the German doctor to save Ellis, speaking of the:

Ausländer-Abteilung Ausschuß für Rat und Hilfe

Ausschuss für deutsche Kriegsgefangene.

EVIDENCE FORM

Name, Surname, Rank: James Clive Lieut ELLIS (INITIALS UNKNOWN).

Regiment, Company (of the missing): TANK CORPS.

Name, Surname, Rank: Lieut O.S.D. WILLS

Regiment, Company Witness: Norfolk Regt. at present at GRAUDENZ Off K-G. LAG.

Date and place of the disappearance: 22 MARCH 1918 near TINCOURT

Particular details: In which circumstance did the Witness see the disappeared for the last time? An Officer of the rank of Lieut in the Tank Corps was seen by me in the 55th Feld Lazarette about April 10th 1918. His name was Ellis. He was badly wounded (fractured left thigh high up, afterwards amputated). He told me he was shot by a sniper after leaving his tank which he had destroyed on the 22nd March.

Was he killed outright? And by whom was he buried? No. After I had left the 55th Feld Lazarette about April 15" at VILLERS-FAUCON, I heard from Officers mentioned below that he had died and was buried in the cemetery just West of the village of VILLERS FAUCON by the Feld Lazarett mentioned, commanded by Oberstabsarzt Dr Frÿ

Can the witness (state the names) of other witnesses? At the same Feld Lazarett were
Capt Monaghan South African Med. Corps (unwounded)
Capt Calmsac R.A.F. (wounded) Lieut Leslie M.Gun Corps

Special Remarks: I am not at all sure that this Officer was named E.C. Ellis. He was tall, thin, with fresh colored complexion large dark eyes, black curly hair, prominent cheek bones, aquiline nose. ~~Oberstabsarzt Dr Frÿ did everything in his power to save this officers life~~

In the presence of the Commandant on: 10/8/18 the

EINLAGE Nº 691

Signature of the witness: Osborne Wills Lieutenant Norfolk Regt.

Form. 380 a a.

Stamp: Geprüft. Offizier-Kriegsgefangenenlager Graudenz P.

The account of Clive Ellis' death from Feld Lazaret 55, written by another Greshamian, Osborne Wills. They do not seem to have realised that they had both attended Gresham's School.

> "...kindness and care of Dr Fry and his staff. The number of wounded was very large, both British and German, and the staff here undoubtedly did their best for us... Conditions were extremely bad owing to the lack of medical personnel, bandages, and sanitary and washing appliances."

No wonder Ellis was a victim of gas gangrene. The shortness of Ellis' active service was reflected in the remarks of his commanding officer, who clearly did not know him at all:

> "Though he was only with the battalion a few days he had already made himself thoroughly popular and was a very promising officer."

For his widowed mother, a Quaker, who had with the greatest restraint and dignity sought news of her only son for over a year, there were to be few mementoes of his last weeks. All his kit and effects were lost "owing to military exigencies". It is to be hoped that Wills' letters to her were at least some small consolation.

The death of Hugh Palmer illustrates the danger that doctors on the front line were in. He had studied medicine at Edinburgh and was married to a doctor whom he presumably met there. At the outbreak of war he had to sell his practice before he could take his commission in November 1914. On the night of 24-25 April 1918, Palmer, by this time a captain in the RAMC and mentioned in despatches, was on duty in an advanced dressing station on the Somme front near the village of Crouy. He had just finished dressing the wounds of two Germans when a shell exploded in the dugout causing him serious injuries. He died the following afternoon.

Only a few days later, on 2 May, this time near Ypres, Norman Procter MC died of wounds suffered in the Battle of Kemmel Hill (29 April). Procter was with the 1/6th Duke of Wellington's West Riding Regiment. Hedley Knowles, who had died in an accident in 1915, had been with the 6th Regiment too, and as both their fathers were Skipton men it seems reasonable to assume that they knew each other before they came to Gresham's. Their names are next to each other in the school register, as they both entered in the summer of 1907. They were together in the Junior School and subsequently in Headmaster's House. Norman Procter had been mentioned in despatches in April 1916 and won his MC for "long continuous service and devotion to duty" in January 1917. At the time of his death he was signal officer to his brigade. His brigadier wrote to Procter's mother thus.

> "My battle headquarters were at a cottage, and we had located the bulk of our personnel in another small house about 150 yards away. There was a terrific bombardment going on, and we suddenly saw that the other house had been hit by a shell and that some signallers were wounded. Your son at once went across to stop an ambulance on the road in order to get them away quickly and unfortunately got hit himself by another shell on the way over. Your son was a model of an English officer and gentleman. As regards his work, I cannot speak too highly of him."

It is disappointing that the tribute to Procter himself is so entirely conventional. Even his friends relied on clichés: "...the life and soul of the mess", "he was always so cheery... a magnificent example," hiding forever the individual character of the man.

At this point the history of the fallen of Gresham's seems to be an account of the deaths of MC winners. As the war went on the honour was given for long service, and in the conditions of the time this does not seem a case of being damned by faint praise. To have survived the unimaginable chaos and slaughter of the key Somme battles, for example, might be thought reason enough to be decorated. Richard Rumsby was a case in point. Commissioned in the Sussex Regiment, he was awarded his MC in 1917 for doing:

> "...valuable work in support of the leading Company, afterwards displaying great skill and initiative in making reconnaissances and collecting men who had gone astray. He has done similar work on previous occasions."

In 1918 Rumsby was transferred to the RFC as an observer with 57th Squadron, and it was in this role that he lost his life near Lens on 9 May. The DH4 in which he was flying was badly shot up and although the pilot managed to return to the aerodrome he crashed on landing and Rumsby died of his injuries.

Coincidentally, the next Gresham's fatality was also that of an observer in the RFC, Douglas Wells, also the possessor of an MC. He was clearly a gifted young man, distinguishing himself both at school and in France. As a boy he had been a school prefect and house captain, about to go up to Cambridge in the autumn of 1914 but instead obtaining a commission in the Lancaster Regiment. He was involved in all the major Somme battles, and was at the taking of Messines Ridge. In 1916 he was mentioned in despatches and in 1917 awarded his MC for "conspicuous gallantry in action and devotion to duty". Having transferred to the

RFC in October 1917, he went to the Front as an observer with 62 Squadron in January 1918, so once again his fellows paid tribute to a man they had known for only a short time. In that short time, however, he had been involved in two hits, the second just the day before he died. His flight commander was perhaps groping for appropriate words as he wrote to Wells' parents, but hit his stride a little better as he went on:

> "Your son was a magnificent shot, and one of the bravest and best observers we ever had, and the very fact of having him and his pilot near me in the flight gave me a feeling of security. I am sure I owe my life to the way they stuck to me in many a tight corner though a less unselfish course might have brought them greater personal success. Your son was a universally loved member of the finest squadron I have been in. Please believe that you have the heartfelt sympathy of one who, working and playing with him for a few short months, feels very deeply the loss of one of the bravest and straightest men he ever met."

Another motif of this period has become apparent – the number of Greshamians who transferred to the RFC. Whether this was because of the horrors of the trenches or because of the glamour of the new technology is not clear. Perhaps both were factors. Certainly by 1918, the air services had grown hugely, with an estimated 2,000-3,000 aeroplanes at the Front in that year. Recruitment was clearly necessary to turn the 300 officers at the start of war into the 27,000 at the end. The other possibly relevant feature is that Gresham's was strong in engineering and produced a number of boys who were keenly interested in that subject.

Alec Malcolm came into the latter category, although he had little time to pursue his interest after school as he did not leave until April 1914 and was commissioned in the Cheshire Yeomanry in June 1915. His service with them included a period of fighting in the Irish rebellion of 1916. After about six months at Sandhurst, Malcolm went to France with the Lancers, seeing action in the German retreat in the Somme area in 1917, after which he volunteered for the RAF and trained as an observer. On 17 May 1918, stationed at Alquines with 98 Squadron, he went out on a high reconnaissance flight in the Ypres-Menin district from which he never returned. It was not until December that he was traced. Wreckage of an aeroplane of the type in which he was flying was identified on the Ypres-Menin road, the official record stating that it had been shot down. There were two graves nearby, marked, "Lieut. Bell and his observer." Lieutenant (or captain) R. W. Bell was Malcolm's pilot. Subsequently the graves were lost, and Alec Malcolm's name appears on the Arras Flying Services Memorial.

Mervyn Trendell was a pilot, this time in the RNAS. He gained his wings, as was proudly reported in the school magazine, being "the only one in his class to have the letters V.G.I. (very good indeed) added to his qualifications". He joined the battle cruiser HMS *Galatea* in February 1918 and was killed as the result of an accident while on duty, in May. He was still only 18. His body was brought home and rests in the churchyard at Upper Sheringham where his father was vicar. His grave has pride of place near the numerous graves of the Upcher family, the local landowners, and is thus very accessible even after so many years have passed.

The pattern of but a short stay at the Front in the bitter fighting of 1918 is repeated in the career of Edmund Prideaux-Brune, a young man who passed in to Sandhurst winning a Prize Cadetship less than two years before he was killed on 22 May 1918. His was a distinguished military background, as both his father and his brother served in the Rifle Brigade. His brother, Colonel Denys Prideaux-Brune, commanded the 13th Battalion Rifle Brigade on the Somme in the dreadful aftermath of High Wood in which so many of his men had been killed. As his new recruits alongside the remaining battle-weary survivors marched out of Albert on 20 July 1916, an officious acting regimental sergeant-major ordered them to "march to attention". Prideaux-Brune, riding in front of them, waved his hand impatiently. "Cut it out, sergeant-major! And the men can smoke if they like." (quoted by Lyn Macdonald, *Somme*) This was, of course, a mightily popular decision, and the picture emerges in another incident, also quoted by Macdonald, of an officer who did not fit the stereotype of a pompous snob. In November of 1916, shortly before the Big Push came officially to its end, Colonel Prideaux-Brune was playing full-back in an Officers v Other Ranks rugby match at the end of a dreary week of preparation for battle. Tackled by a corporal, he was brought down and broke his collarbone, at a most unpropitious moment considering the imminence of the next attack. His younger brother had not the opportunity to make such a mark on the 3rd Battalion Rifle Brigade, as he had been in France only a few weeks when he fell to a bomb from an aeroplane. He was only 19 years old.

An anonymous contributor to *The Gresham* provides one of the few dissonant notes to emerge from a school magazine that kept the patriotic "play the game" spirit alive to a surprising extent as the war entered such a critical stage in 1918. Yet even that moment of discord was turned triumphantly to good account as the moral of the tale unfolded. It is too neat an account to be fully satisfying, and begs too many questions, but parts of it have the ring of truth and the power to move today. Entitled "The Antidote", it begins thus:

> "It is ten o'clock at night, rain is falling and it will be a long time before I reach home. I am in a bad temper. The utter futility of the war and the discomfort we suffer in England make me, for one selfish moment, an ardent pacifist. Here I am in the middle of a large town in England and in pitch darkness – I run into a lamp-post – why don't they allow us to use lights on a night like this? No sensible German would leave the Fatherland..."

The writer sees lights ahead and a stream of ambulances moving towards the railway station. They stop to load up their burden, the first group the stretcher cases. Some are not expected to survive:

> "Next come the men who are able to move and talk. They are laid in rows on the pavement, and put, one by one into the cars. I notice that almost all are smoking, and very cheerful. One of them asks me for a cigarette. I obtain one and offer it to him, wondering why he does not take it. 'Put it in my mouth,' he says quite simply, 'I have lost both my arms.' I do so and light it with a shaking hand."

This, of course, is the moment of guilt for earlier unpatriotic sentiments.

Alleyne Boxall's letters of spring and summer 1918 mention the deaths of some of his former schoolfellows and reveal that Howson, despite continuing ill health, was keeping in touch with his former pupil. "He has not been very well but he is picking up again," commented Boxall at the end of May 1918. Boxall received *The Times*, recently increased in price from 2d to 3d, on a regular basis, and the newspapers as well as letters from school seem to have kept him well informed. He knew of Prideaux-Brune's death – "Do you remember him? He used to play the piano very well at Holt." – and commented that Chapman and Malcolm were missing, although Boxall was optimistic that they would turn up amongst the ranks of prisoners. By 1 July he was in aggressive mood:

"Lull before the storm," "Allies awaiting the next move" – nice things to read in the trenches, especially front line, by moonlight. "I'll see every devil is killed that comes near me or this company. I'm not half up against them at present."

By now the shortage of cigarettes was such that Mrs Boxall was sending them from home. "One has to run round to no end of shops before one finds any." Despite that annoyance, "The Americans are a very good lot – and awfully jolly."

As Gresham's was a small school it has been tempting to use the surviving photographs to deduce where possible the names of boys where they are not actually given. Using school lists and record books, a good deal of knowledge of some individuals emerges, and if they belonged to a small group such as the school prefects it is possible, by a process of elimination, to identify some boys with a degree of certainty. One such is Arthur Estcourt. Much is known about his background and his military career, but his final resting-place remained mysterious.

The Commonwealth War Graves Commission's massive list of 1.7 million of the fallen in the two world wars yielded no record under that name and spelling, and although various alternatives and possibilities were suggested, no answer was forthcoming for many months. It seemed he might have changed his name, although certainly the school knew nothing of it and there is no known reason for it. The name Eastcote suddenly appears on the third sheet of his service record at the Public Record Office, with the original name scribbled out – although it is given as "Estcourt" on the first sheet of the documents and reappears as such on the fourth sheet. The name "Eastcote" did not produce any information from the CWGC either. The War Office was unsure about his rank at the time of his death, giving him the rank of "Captain", then deleting that and replacing it with "Lieut". He was given temporary rank occasionally and sometimes commanded the 58th Trench Mortar Battery which may explain the confusion. There is a document clearly stating that he gave up the rank of captain in August 1917, reverting to "T 2nd Lieut". However, all the records relating to his transfer to the RFC in February 1918 give him the rank of captain. The issue may not be very important in itself, but it does reflect the mysterious nature of the record.

The story is a familiar one. Arthur Estcourt did well at Gresham's and went up to Magdalene College, Cambridge, on a Mathematical Scholarship in 1912. He was with the Gloucesters when he won an MC in 1916:

> "He fought his battery with great effect under very heavy fire during the attack, (at La Boisselle, during the Battle of the Somme) dispersing many enemy bombing parties. He also knocked out a machine-gun which was holding up the advance of one of our bombing parties."

According to a letter written at the time by his commanding officer, Estcourt:

> "...directed the fire of the Battery with great accuracy from a very exposed position under heavy fire. It was entirely due to his great coolness that several bombing parties were dispersed... He also greatly distinguished himself at Bazentin-le-Petit [*where Mark Hill was killed*]."

In August 1916 he was wounded in both thighs by sniper's bullets, and was at home until December. The following August he was one of the men severely injured – this time in the right knee – by the premature explosion of a defective bomb which killed one of his comrades, and once again was invalided back to England until the end of the year. Maybe this enforced period of rest enabled him to think about the future or maybe he had simply had enough of being injured in trench warfare, but at any rate he began to train with the RFC, passing out at the head of the list in the Flying School Examination in April 1918. Sent to the Front in May as an observer with 5th Squadron, he went out on morning contact patrol in an RE8 over enemy lines on 8 August, and he and his pilot were both found dead "later". At this point – silence. A special search was necessary before the CWGC was able finally to establish Estcourt's resting place – a well-marked grave rather than a mention on a memorial – at Caix, on the Somme, about 28 kilometres south-east of Amiens.

A Marvellous Change for the Better?

AT GRESHAM'S the end of the academic year had been celebrated on Speech Day on 28 July 1918. Howson spoke, amongst other things, of his pride in the School Cadet Force, and of his hope that a war memorial would be provided for the chapel in the form of stalls, panelling and screen. He expressed his delight at seeing the governors once again at Speech Day "especially when rail travel is such a penance". But he ended on a familiar theme, that of the Old Boys:

> "One of the most gratifying facts in the life of the school is that Old Boys show such a deep attachment to and great unflagging interest in the school. They do not forget. Nor could we forget. They have not fallen short of the fine standards set by the English Public School boy of High heart, high speech, high deeds, Mid honouring eyes."

This summarised Howson's philosophy for Gresham's and was the validation of his life's work, but the price paid in war had been high. Certificates were issued for the first time in those days of necessary war economy and deftly defended by Sir Edward Busk, the chairman of the governors:

> "We shall bear in mind that the Greeks, whose civilisation was probably the highest and most intellectual the world has ever known, made a practice of awarding wreaths and other prizes of no intrinsic value, deeming that success was the only honour worth considering."

Sir Edward, too, paid tribute to the training of Gresham's OTC, linking it with the honours won by those under arms.

> "So far as can be ascertained there are 467 Old Gresham (*sic*) boys now serving of whom 413 are officers and 54 are of other ranks.

> The following are the total distinctions won since the beginning of the War – DSO 3 and 1 Bar, MC 46 and 1 Bar, DSC 2, DFC 1, MM 2, Foreign Decorations 10, Mentioned in Despatches 35. These distinctions, numbering over 100, are an exceptionally high percentage of the entire number of Old Boys known to have served and the school has obviously gained a very high place for efficiency and courage.
>
> With grief, but yet with pride, we note that during the war 85 Old Boys and 1 Master have been killed."

Busk may have been on firmer ground when he was speaking of the school's war record than he was in imagining the likely relationship of Greshamians with their men in wartime circumstances. In a passage of staggering patronage he described the benefits of a Gresham's education:

> "Notwithstanding that education has for many years been compulsory and free, yet it has not had the expected effect, and men who join the army are found to require even elementary instruction and to find it very difficult to learn. Old Greshamians, when they perceive this will be able to say to the men, 'Why, we learned this when we were at school or at college.' You will then be able to explain matters to them in an informal and friendly way, to remove their difficulties and to smooth their way to further progress."

Noblesse oblige indeed!

Back on the Somme, by August 1918 the battle lines were much as they had been in 1916. Guy Tyler fell in action on the 22nd after a varied military career spanning almost all of the war. In August 1914 he had immediately joined the quaintly-named Artists' Rifles, part of the Territorial Force, and went to France in October. In November, after the First Battle of Ypres, Sir John French offered a number of commissions to the Artists' in the old line regiments of the famous "First Seven Divisions" which had taken so much punishment in the first few months of the war. Guy Tyler accepted one of them, and after training in France he took a commission in the Norfolk Regiment, although he was not a native of the county. Early in the war he was a keen correspondent and his letters to the school are some of the best. He wrote about that period of time when the Artists' had taken commissions in other regiments:

> "The Artists' men who have taken commissions are naturally

> suffering very severely, because every single one has gone straight into the firing line, and a great number that I knew, both at home and in the Artists' afterwards, have been killed. I believe that of the first 50 to go through the school of instruction with me over half are already casualties."

Tyler was in the trenches around Ypres until 30 May 1915, when he was severely wounded by a rifle bullet in the right shoulder, in which a portion of the scapula was destroyed. The injury healed but the damage to the movement of the shoulder joint was permanent and for over a year he was in England recuperating. In January 1917, still unfit for active service, and unable to raise his right arm even to shoulder level, he applied for a wound pension, which he received, and volunteered for base work abroad. He was put in command of a prisoner-of-war company in France. His letter to school gives, as was usual with Guy Tyler, a good deal of information and his forthright viewpoint:

> "A Prisoners of War Company consists of two English Officers, an escort and 450 German prisoners of all ranks below officers. The prisoners are kept in the same Company as much as possible, and my company has just been celebrating (quel mot) the anniversary of its formation, the greater part having been captured at Courcellette in September 1916. On formation a Company is given one or two German Sgt. Majors, eight corporals, six interpreters, a certain number of carpenters and other useful men, a few medical men, and the rest labourers. They then have the whole organisation complete, and the Company can be divided into Platoons and Squads under the NCOs just like a British Company.
>
> The bulk of the prisoners work all day, road-making, railway-making, quarrying etc., and are in an extremely fit condition. They get good food – as good as our own troops – and have a canteen in their compound supplied by goods from English canteens. They have money sent from Germany and also receive working pay for all days on which they work. They also have a large supply of parcels from Germany, the most common contents being black bread, tobacco and cigarettes, though they contain many other things.
>
> Their chief amusements – besides eating – are singing and playing on musical instruments, partly home-made, and partly from Germany. The choirs practise with great thoroughness and are very good, while my Company has a really brilliant string band.

Melville Royds-Jones.

> There are some very clever craftsmen amongst them, and, if you are able to turn them on to their own trades, they take a great delight in their work.
>
> Of course we get a lot of jeers for treating them so well, but they are very well-behaved and give no trouble at all, and it is not usual with us as a nation to kick a man when he is down. That is what it comes to."

When Guy Tyler finally recovered from his injuries he rejoined the Norfolks and went to Italy, where he was commended for some splendid map-making. Returning to France in April 1918, he was killed by a shell during a German counter-attack. Apparently his work the previous day, when the battalion was attacked in a fog, would have led to a recommendation for an honour had he lived. Unusually, among the customary remarks about cheerfulness so often adduced in tributes, his chaplain, whom he knew well, spoke of his "quiet devotion to duty" and concluded:

> "I am only one of many who will not forget his gallantry and his patience as long as I live."

There are very few of the Gresham's fallen whose personal letters survive, but thanks to Dr Jonathan Royds-Jones there is a record of a correspondence between his father, E. Melville Royds-Jones, and his close friend Harry Bartleet. Both left school early to join up. They had been in the same house at school and kept up their friendship until Harry was killed in France in 1918. Harry Bartleet provides an example of the young men who were sent out to France after a few months training and plunged into front-line leadership. To battle-scarred veterans in the ranks, in very much depleted numbers in 1918, they must have seemed mere schoolboys, which is in effect what they were. Harry Bartleet was only 19. Despite the shortage of men at the Front, he trained at Blackdown for about five months before he went with the London Rifle Brigade to the Peronne area in August. The expressions of disillusionment from war poets later famous found no resonance here. This young man, from May onwards, was longing to be sent to the Front, and grew increasingly bored at Blackdown. At the end of June he wrote:

> "I am still here doing practically nothing. I have a platoon which I inspect each morning, and that is practically all I can do with them, for all their training is done by specialist instructors and I can only look on and get fed up."

Harry Bartleet. Bartleet was killed in his first action in September 1918 aged only 19. Royds-Jones described his friend's death as "a tragedy he thought he would never get over".

His last letter is dated 22 July and he was still frustrated.

> "I am very fed up indeed as I am sure you would be under the circumstances for I have been put on battle Surplus and cannot possibly get off it. The Battn. expect to move very soon and while they are having a good scrap I shall be messing about behind doing p.t. or musketry! If I had been in a show I should not mind but to come out here and be put behind for the first show is the limit. We seem to have Jerry properly on toast now, quite in the cart I should say."

Ironically he was killed in his eagerly-awaited first action on 19 September at Epehy, the village being regained for the Allies on 18 September. Mortally wounded by a sniper, he died of his wounds about two hours later.

> "All the men speak of his gallant behaviour, especially as it was his first time in action... During the attack he showed great courage and good leadership. His men say that he was absolutely fearless."

These comments by his superiors meant a great deal to Harry Bartleet's mother.

> "Dear Melville,
>
> We were so pleased to get a kind sympathy letter from one who knew our dear Harry so well; I believe you will be genuinely sorry to lose him as a friend. It is a terrible blow to us, particularly as we were looking forward to his being with us now his school days were over. But such was not to be and I am trying to realise that it must be for the best – that he was taken so young – but it is difficult.
>
> He was in France only 5 or 6 weeks and was killed in his first action, going over with the 5th London. His Major in writing to us says his men say he was 'absolutely fearless' when he led them. From his Captain we hear that his platoon was in advance of the rest, showing that he was not wanting in courage. I thought this would be his attitude when in action, as although quiet and reserved, he had considerable strength of character when put to the test. He had also a strong sense of his duty in getting over to France at the earliest possible date."

Hannah Bartleet's surmise that Melville Royds-Jones would be sorry to lose his friend proved an understatement. His son wrote in 1999:

> "I remember my father telling me that when he was young he suffered a personal tragedy that he thought he would never get over. He would never elaborate on it. It was only after his death that I discovered these letters – I think this was the tragedy."

The war was coming to a sooner than expected end for Alleyne Boxall too. It is sometimes tempting to feel that with strawberries for tea, champagne, *The Times*, a kind and attentive mother sending parcels from home and the company of like-minded friends that Boxall had an easy war. Such, however, was not the case. Not only had he lost several of his closest friends, but he also was repeatedly wounded, and his courage was such that he made light of such incidents. On 25 September 1918 he wrote to his mother:

> "I've not the energy to write much at present but just a line to let you know I was wounded yesterday at about 5.0am by a wizz-bang...It's a marvel how I'm here to tell the tale... The worst wound I have is one on the left side, just below the 7th rib. I've also got the following, but don't worry as I'm all right and they are mostly not much more than scratches although I'm bandaged from head to foot!!! Starting at the top and working downwards – forehead, below left eye, face and neck all scratches, left shoulder, left side, left leg (approximate number 10!!) Right leg, right foot. Both arms, left hand – so you can see I must be a picture. However it's marvellous I can sit up and have resumed my normal appetite...I shan't half require some clothes when I arrive the other side, you see it will take my valise about 3 to 4 weeks to get over. And absolutely everything I had on had to be burnt as they were all covered with blood. Including that wonderful pair of socks, knitted with three different wools. Well here is the doctor so must steady up – otherwise I might get into trouble for writing!"

Alfred Hyde, a pupil of John Chambré Miller in Farfield, had after some difficulty joined the RAF and was killed in late September 1918. Chambré Miller had made out a very good case for his acceptance in the following terms. "Mechanical tastes. Athletic. Cool and reliable. Very fair initiative." But in 1917 this fair-haired, blue-eyed slender young man was rejected when he approached the medical board of the RFC, presumably too slight for their liking at 5ft 7½ins but weighing only 9st 2lbs. Given that he was rejected, he was described, rather mystifyingly, as "of the strenuous type". He must have been disappointed, but less than two weeks later his application was accepted and in February 1918, Alfred Hyde gained the long-awaited temporary commission. In April he wrote from Catterick a modest letter to his much-liked housemaster Chambré Miller and his wife. By this time he had gained full acceptance into the RFC and was in his words "no longer on probation". His admission that "flying seems to me to be very tiring", suggests that he may not have been of the most robust sort. On 8 September he wrote his last letter back to school. Again he spoke of tiredness after four days completing two raids a day, but confidently of British air superiority:

Alfred Hyde, proudly wearing the uniform of the RAF. It seems that the badge might have been added to the photograph after it was taken.

> "There seem to be a lot of Boches on this front but they are being well looked after by our own scout machines and are undoubtedly coming off 2nd best. We get quite a lot of fighting ourselves but our casualties are very light as we usually have an escort and we have to keep the Hun off until the escort can get amongst them."

He described an exciting occasion when he and his observer met nine German scout planes as they were returning from a reconnaissance flight and, thanks to Hyde's skill in throwing the machine around, escaped them. Later he was complimented by his CO and commented:

> "After a scrap like that you feel what a splendid thing it is to live… I was told by one of the fellows here that we are evidently not going to be killed in this war if we got through that lot all right."

Hyde looked forward to his next leave in eight or nine weeks time, and signed off with kind regards to all at Gresham's. Two weeks later he was killed, his commanding officer being of the sort who believed in being cruel to be kind.

> "I am very, very sorry to tell you that your boy failed to return from a bomb raid last night. I am afraid that I can't give you very much hope either, as the machine was shot to pieces and then caught fire and fell in little bits. I am afraid it sounds horribly brutal but it is better for you to know than to hold out a hope that all may be well."

Significantly, this part of the letter was not printed in *The Times* nor, therefore, in the school magazine. The lines that followed, about his cheerful fearlessness, were all faithfully reproduced, but the details of his fate were too harrowing for public consumption, even though his father had been spared nothing. These omitted remarks provide a reminder about the possible incompleteness of public records of the time. For Alfred's elder brother, Tom, also an OG, there was a happy ending, however, for in 1924 he married the Chambré Millers' eldest daughter, Madge.

Fifteen boys had joined Gresham's School in the summer of 1906. Among them were Mark Hill, Guy Tyler and Keith Batten. Tyler, who was only three months older than Batten, and who left school in the same year, 1909, predeceased his former classmate by only six months. Batten, training to be a solicitor, was also a Territorial officer at the outbreak of war, and had been mobilised on 4 August 1914. He met his death emerging first from a trench, leading his men as a captain with the Bedfordshire Regiment on 27 September 1918. Hit by a shell, he died instantaneously. The chaplain wrote warmly and personally of him:

> "He was a splendid fellow, always cheery and with a wonderful humour all his own. I found him a great help and we were great friends."

It is well to remember that some men really were the cheerful souls their fellows claimed them to be.

By August 1918 the tide was certainly turning, bearing out Harry Bartleet's words about the Germans being "quite in the cart". John Nicholson was fighting in France in the Pas de Calais, near Grevillers, which had been recaptured from the Germans by the New Zealand Division on 24 August. Having survived the battles for Bourlon Wood, part of the Cambrai attack and the March retreat, Nicholson died of wounds received in action on 5 October 1918.

Leslie Davies MC, pictured with the 8th Battalion Norfolk Regiment. He died one day before the war ended, of malaria, in Beirut.

Far away from the Western Front, in the Middle East, another OG was dying, but this time slowly. Leslie Davies MC was a major in the Norfolk Regiment attached to a cavalry regiment of the Machine Gun Corps. His family lived in Antingham Rectory, North Walsham, only a few miles from Holt, as his father was a clergyman. After Gresham's he had studied at Emmanuel College, Cambridge, taking his degree in June 1914, only weeks before the war broke out. From July 1915 he had been in France, winning his Military Cross in the Somme Offensive in 1916. At the Battle of Thiepval in September, he organised a party of men to bring up rations, the usual system having failed. This involved a journey to the Advanced Report Centre with pack ponies, described by his colonel as "a very difficult and dangerous operation owing to very heavy hostile shell fire". Three days later, when the Royal West Surrey Regiment was reported as being short of SAA and grenades, Davies formed a group of reserve Lewis gunners and brought the weapons and ammunition through an intense artillery barrage. Finally in early October, at the Schwaben Redoubt, he handled his guns superbly, although two of them were knocked out and he himself was wounded in the neck. After being wounded again he joined the army in Palestine, achieving the rank of major in June 1918. Wrote his Brigadier-General after his death:

"It is especially cruel that he should fall a victim to malaria just at the finish of the war. He had been so plucky throughout these last operations. He was far from well nearly the whole time, but refused to go sick and ran his show splendidly in spite of the strain he must have been under the whole time."

Davies succumbed to malaria on 10 November 1918, one day before the Armistice, and is buried in Beirut Cemetery.

In Holt, at school, celebrations of the end of the war were sober. The official notification of the Armistice reached Holt by means of a telegram displayed in the window of the Post Office. Howson sent a prefect down to the town, which was normally out of bounds to the boys, to confirm that the news was genuine. At midday on 11 November, all the boys were summoned to Big School where the headmaster told them of the Armistice. Three cheers and the singing of the first verse of the National Anthem followed. The boys were given a half-day holiday, and in the afternoon the OTC paraded, celebrating the signing of the Armistice by a "Feu de Joie" fired with blank cartridges over the playing fields. However, the joy was muted by the memory of "those who have not lived to see this day". The next morning at 9am, the school went to chapel for a Thanksgiving Service, at which special hymns and chants were sung, including a solemn Te Deum. Howson's address came from the *Book of Revelation.* He spoke of the "unequalled sacrifice of the gallant dead," quoting the words,

"Great is our inheritance
When heroes die."

Speaking of those who had died, he said: "Those of us who knew them will never forget what they were to us." But he, like all good schoolmasters, looked forward, in this case to the making of "a new world" which would be in the hands of the boys before him rather than in his own. *His* time was running out.

The townspeople of Holt, and army units billeted in and around the Old School House in the centre of town, were much more ebullient than the school community. Once again motor-cycles were careering around. Wynne Willson, who liked to wear cricket gear for the house photograph, and who was certainly an aficionado of the noble game, became very worried that the cyclists would damage the wicket!

Si monumentum requiris, circumspice

BY THE end of the war, Howson's health was failing again. The last house photograph of him taken in July 1918 shows that the once stocky figure was much reduced. It must have been a blessed relief to him that the lists of the dead would not be much further lengthened, and that the weekly intercessions in chapel could come to an end. But the losses had been great – by that time almost 100 men had fallen from a school which in 1914 had numbered under 250. By January 1919, Howson was once again seriously ill, although determinedly carrying on with his work. The end came suddenly, and to many, unexpectedly. The school was closed for the Christmas holiday and the headmaster was in London at the beginning of the month for meetings of the HMC and the Gresham's War Memorial Committee, but he was too ill to attend them. He asked to be taken home to Holt, which he was. Two days later, on 7 January, he was dead. His death certificate gives the cause of death as "chronic nephritis and degeneration of the heart muscle". After his death the tributes, of course, flowed in. His funeral was held in the chapel which "was very near his heart", and he was buried in a brick grave lined with laurel leaves near the south wall. The inscription reads, "He being dead yet speaketh." On the step at the foot of the grave, at the request of his sister, Rosa, are carved the words "Amor Vincit Omnia."

Remarks were made at that time which suggest that the war broke Howson. This may have been a romanticised view, but a number of his contemporaries suggested it. It is beyond doubt that he had given his time and interest to the boys to an extraordinary degree. Some who were lost in the war had moved with him to the new school in 1903, and to those boys he was particularly close. They had been pioneers together, working to establish Howson's vision of Gresham's as a unique school, and the bond between them was strong. A friend's obituary in *The Times* made the point well.

> "In a very unusual degree Mr Howson took a personal interest in the boys, and made them feel that after they had left it was a real

The last school photograph of George Howson, taken in July 1918. Illness, and perhaps grief, visibly aged him, and his stocky frame is much diminished.

> pleasure to him to see them back; so that school became a home and centre to old boys in a way which is certainly unusual, and in the writer's experience, unique."

This same friend wrote that Howson had been "greatly distressed" by the death of so many old boys in the war.

In Howson's memorial service, held on 2 February, his old friend, the Bishop of Thetford in his address asked:

> "Cannot you picture him, proudly standing at the head of his heroic Gresham boys, who have fallen in the war, and looking up to God and saying, 'Behold me and the children whom thou hast given me.'"

The bishop also paid tribute to Howson's legendary excellence as a host.

> "Whenever I came to visit the School for a Confirmation Service there was no question of arriving at the Front door of the School House and ringing the bell. As soon as my train got into Holt, there he was on the platform to greet me."

The biographical memoir published anonymously in the school magazine refers to:

> "...the storm of war... stabbing again and again as one after another his best-honoured boys were taken, and there is no doubt that his severe illness was hastened by his poignant distress.
> What his old boys were to him and he to them may partly be judged by the enormous correspondence, the unfailing touch he kept with them, the wonderful welcome he gave them, by the confidences they entrusted to him, and the constant stream that came back to him. During the war there was hardly a single week in which some Old Boy was not staying here, perhaps as many as five or six at a time, who would save for the school a few days from their hard-earned leave: back like homing pigeons from all over the world. That was surely his great reward. No wonder he was hard hit. The way he would speak of them in Chapel, for all its restraint, revealed how deep was the stress."

Percy Hooper, aged about 17 in 1903.

For one OG there was a particular memory of a remark Howson made:

> "...I can't sleep in my comfortable bed – I feel it ought to be a trench... He must have suffered horribly through the war, by the loss of so many whom he loved, by the feeling of helplessness in the face of all the pain it involved for others, and by the world-wide downfall of ideals which he had devoted his life to building up in the school."

Edith, the Duchess of Hamilton, who had given out the prizes on Speech Day in 1915 and who presumably knew Howson reasonably well, was even more direct:

> "The War killed him as straightly and surely as if he had fallen at the Front."

Of course, for many men the war had not completely ended on 11 November. Thousands stayed under arms, and continued to carry out military duties. One such was Percy Hooper. Hooper seems to have been an unusual character, with two strong and almost opposing sides to his nature. He had gone to a public school in England, of course, proceeded to Selwyn College, Cambridge, then moved to Canada. There was nothing extraordinary about any of that, but when he arrived in the New World his career choices were perhaps surprising. He lived for a while in the United States where he worked as a poultry farmer in California, and by October 1915 when he joined up, he was back in Canada, in Toronto, working as a waiter. There is no photograph of him as an adult, but his medical history form shows him to have been a small man, 5ft 2ins tall with a chest measurement of 30ins. For a man of his age, even early in the 20th century, that would have been a slight figure. His age, actually, is another unusual feature. He signed various forms at the time of his enlistment which give his age as 26, whereas according to school registration documents he was 29. The reason for such an action on his part is not clear. He may have wanted to appear younger than he actually was at an earlier stage in his career in America or Canada, perhaps to secure a job, then later had to make the facts fit. In June 1916 he came to England on the SS *Olympic*, the sister ship to the *Titanic*, with the 95th Battalion of the Canadian Infantry and a matter of only days after went to France. He was wounded in the upper right arm at Vimy Ridge in April 1917. Subsequently he was offered a commission, but, predictably, preferred to stay in the ranks, receiving the rank of corporal. His fate was that of tens of thousands

in 1919 and 1920. He fell ill while at Witley Camp, Bramshott, and died two days later of influenza, described as "serious case of toxic type, with marked cyanosis," on his hospital record.

It was not until July 1919, after the official signing of the peace treaty at Versailles on 28 June, that a dinner at school was given to the 180 or so returning soldiers and sailors of Gresham's to give thanks for peace and their safe return. The dinner was the final event of two days' celebration, consisting of a holiday for the schoolboys so that they could treat the OGs to cricket matches, a swimming relay, a shooting competition and a performance of *A Midsummer Night's Dream* in the theatre in the woods. There was also a chapel service on 1 July, the anniversary of the first day of the Somme battle, especially moving for some of the old boys who had not, of course, seen the chapel in its completed state:

> "To many of us it was the first sight of the chapel, and mingled with this was the poignant feeling that there were some who would never see it, and above all, of one who would have loved to welcome us to the chapel, for which he had worked so hard… No hymns can ever be so inspiring as when sung by such a brotherhood as this…For the splendid but terrible list of the fallen there are no adequate words."

Mr Wynne Willson was called upon to make a speech at the OG dinner; the sentiments expressed indicative of some of the dislocation peace brought:

> "For five years the nation – the world – has been in the throes of fever and delirium. Now it is convalescent, and like convalescents it is somewhat fractious and peevish… Let none of us throw away the patience, the brotherliness, the sanity, the unselfishness that drew the nation together till Victory."

Wynne Willson wrote in his memoir:

> "For my own Junior House I made an illuminated war memorial containing the names of all the Old Boys killed who had been in the Junior House, and opposite each name I put in a circle the boy's head taken from the House group when he was 13 or 14, made in many cases 10 or 15 years before. Those little boys' faces in that memorial always seemed to me infinitely pathetic."

The oak screen commemorating all but one of the fallen of Gresham's, installed in the school chapel in March 1920. The last Greshamian to die as a result of injuries in the war, Henry Vallancey, MC, is not included. He died two months later.

Wynne Willson's son commented in 1999: "He took ages planning and executing it, and it hung in the main dining room [*of Old School House*]."

The memorial, on vellum and much damaged, still exists today, the portraits of some of the children faded or even disappeared. The pathos remains.

This was the time for memorials, and plans for commemoration of the fallen had already been established by the end of the war. Gradually they began to come to fruition. The oak stalls, which bear the names of George Howson and of many of the men killed in the war, were installed in the chapel in March 1920. The screen too was carved and "completed" two months before the very last death of an OG attributable at least in part to the war occurred. Henry Vallancey MC died on 4 May 1920. In September 1916 he had received a severe gunshot wound to the face resulting in the loss of his left eye and was awarded the MC in 1917, relinquishing his commission with honorary rank in June 1918. Despite his injury, after the war he was able to return to work as a colliery contractor's manager. The cause of his death was firstly pneumococcal meningitis, from which he had suffered for only two and a half days, but the wound he had sustained was mentioned secondly on his death certificate.

The school, of course, took up the challenge of post-war life wholeheartedly under the leadership of James Eccles, who worked faithfully to continue the precepts of Howson for the next generation. The 1920s proved a dynamic period, with two of the greatest names in the arts of the 20th century, W. H. Auden and Benjamin Britten both in Farfield House during that decade. But Howson's death so soon after the Armistice marked the end of a distinctive era in the life of the school.

The final roll of honour of Gresham's School comprises 101 names – 100 old boys and one master killed out of a serving group of about 500. The worst "snapshot" of the death toll of Gresham's was that of the summer term 1911. That term there were 201 boys on the school roll, of whom 45 were to die in the war. But that figure conceals much greater losses in some groups. Of the tiny Upper Sixth, four out of seven lost their lives, as did 12 out of a fifth form of 24 – a truly shocking statistic. Of course, other public schools suffered similar losses of similar lieutenants and second-lieutenants, exposed to maximum danger while leading their men into battles dominated by a weight of firepower such as the world had never before seen and against which the human frame was pitifully inadequate. But the spirit and resolution of this small, close-knit group of young men from an unusual school tucked away in the remoteness of North Norfolk lives on powerfully. Each day, present Greshamians sit in the memorial chapel so many of the serving soldiers never saw, but which is rich in reminders of their contribution to and their belief in the "Great War for Civilisation". Above all, Howson's boys live still through letters to a headmaster whose fate was bound up with their own and whose heroes they most emphatically were.

A Postscript

THERE are some names on the vellum memorial from Gresham's Junior School in Old School House which do not appear on the official Gresham's memorial to the fallen of the Great War. These are the names of several boys who left the junior school and did not attend the senior school, or if they did, only very briefly. It is not always clear what happened to them between their departure from Gresham's and their death in war.

There are divided opinions as to whether they should be added to the official figure of Gresham's losses, and there are strong arguments both for and against. The men should at least be mentioned here. They are listed in alphabetical order:

Archibald Keltie Gilmour, a captain with the King's Own Scottish Borderers, died on 16 August 1916 and is buried at Dartmoor Cemetery, on the Somme. He was a Londoner, and returned to his roots after his brief exile in Norfolk from September 1904 to December 1905, attending Westminster School and Balliol College, Oxford. He was in Woodlands. He became a student of the Middle Temple, clearly hoping to follow in the footsteps of his barrister father, and was 24 when he died.

Less is known of Alexander John Hanmer MC, a second-lieutenant with the Buffs, died on 7 October 1916, of wounds received in action on 2 August, aged 20. One of five Greshamian brothers, he was only at the school from January 1908 until April 1909, when he went to Tonbridge School. According to *The Gazette*: "He was in command of a party detailed to capture an advanced position. Having accomplished his task he continued to advance, bombing the enemy until he fell wounded." A native of Kent, he is buried in St Sever Cemetery, Rouen.

Charles Sherriff Ranson was a second-lieutenant with the City of London Regiment, who died near Ypres on 16 August 1917, aged 21. A native of Norwich, he was at school in Norfolk for two years, 1906-1908. I am indebted to Mr Jeremy Francis for the following details about him. He entered St Edward's School, Oxford, in the Summer Term of 1909, was captain of the 1st XV and the cricket team, and became head of school, leaving in 1915. He is commemorated on the Menin Gate Memorial to the Missing.

Also serving near Ypres in 1917 was William Lisle Rockley MC, a native of the city of Nottingham. He joined the school in January 1906 at the same time as Ranson, but stayed for only a few months. Of the 13 boys who came to Gresham's in that cohort, six lost their lives in war. Rockley was 21 when he died on 11

October 1917, and has no known grave, his name being recorded on the Tyne Cot Memorial to the Missing.

Jack Sykes became a lieutenant in the 48th Squadron of the Royal Air Force. He was at Gresham's between 1911 and 1913, and was only 19 when he was killed on 3 October 1918. Born at Windsor, his last resting-place is in the Dadizelle New British Cemetery, West-Vlaanderen in Belgium.

One master, who had taught at Gresham's between 1911 and 1912, also lost his life in the war. He was Geoffrey Reynolds Day, who went from the school to be a Fellow in History of Emmanuel College, Cambridge. He was serving with the Bedfordshire Regiment when he was killed on Sunday, 27 August 1916 on the Somme aged 28, leaving a young widow, Jane. He had previously received a broken jaw and other wounds at Suvla Bay. An officer who was in the next bed to him in hospital spoke of "his amazing fortitude in bearing intense suffering". *The Gresham* described him as: "An able and inspiring teacher, gifted with a keen sense of humour and an attractive personality." His name appears, with those of some of the boys he taught, on the Thiepval Memorial.

Killed in Action
1914 - 1918

Andrews, E.C
Armitage, S.W.
Atkin, G.D.H.
Aveling, L.N.
Ayris, N.
Barker, A.S.
Barker, C.N.
Barker, C.W.T.
Barker, H.F.
Barratt, G.R.
Bartleet, H.B.
Batten, J.K.
Beck, J.S.
Beeton, R.H.
Berridge, R.W.
Biden, L.T.G.V.
Bird, A.C.
Blackburne, E.
Booth, B.B.
Brownsword, D.A.
Busk, H.A.
Carnegie, D.A.
Chapman, H.E.
Chestney, F.W.
Cobon, H.G.
Cole, A.H.
Cornish, B.G.
Crick, C.G.
Crosse, M.E.B.
Crosse, E.C.M.
Cunnell, D.C.
Davies, L.F.St.J.
Drey, A
Duff Gordon, C.L.
Dulley, D.C.C.
Dye, G.H.
Ellis, J.C.
Elwell, E.E.
Estcourt, A.C.
Evans, P.H.
Fenchelle, G.J.
Foster. J.M.
Fox, C.E.
Frost, G.K.
Giles, G.E.
Gissing, W.L.
Goodall, G.M.L,
Graves, A.H.
Halsey, F.W.
Harvey Jones, F.M.
Hawksley, G.
Herron, A.R.
Hill, C.A.
Hill, M.C.
Holland, A.L.
Hooper, P.J.
Hyde, A.N.
Inglis, R.
Jacques, D.W.
Jarvis, A.B.
Johnson, G.B.
Kempson, J.R.
Kirch, C.
Knowles, H.
Malcolm, A.A.
Marriott, S.G.
Mobbs, E.S.
Neal, A.B.
Newsum, C.N.
Nicholson, J.A.
Palmer, H.S.
Partridge, R.H.
Phillimore, J.P.
Preston, S.
Prideaux Brune, E.N.
Procter, J.N.W.A.
Richardson, D.B.
Robinson, H.H.K.
Rogers, D.S.
Rumsby, R.W.
Russell, H.B.
Scott Holmes, H.F.
Shaw, C.F.
Shepherd, C.A.
Sillem, T.G.
Simpson, J.H.
Smith, V.N. (Staff)
Soman, L.A.
Spurrell, F.J.D
Thicknesse, R.S.
Thorn, H.
Trendell, M.H.W.
Tyler, G.C.
Vallancey, H.H.D.
Walker, F.C.
Warwick, J.D.B.
Wells, C.D.
White, E.G.
Wills, A.L.
Wilson, I.M.
Wright, J.M.S.

Index